# Turkish
# Delight
# &
# Treasure
# Hunts

# Turkish Delight & Treasure Hunts

*Delightful Treats and Games*
*from Classic Children's Books*

Jane Brocket

A PERIGEE BOOK

A PERIGEE BOOK
Published by the Penguin Group
Penguin Group (USA) Inc.
375 Hudson Street, New York, New York 10014, USA

Penguin Group (Canada), 90 Eglinton Avenue East, Suite 700, Toronto, Ontario M4P 2Y3, Canada
(a division of Pearson Penguin Canada Inc.)
Penguin Books Ltd., 80 Strand, London WC2R 0RL, England
Penguin Group Ireland, 25 St. Stephen's Green, Dublin 2, Ireland (a division of Penguin Books Ltd.)
Penguin Group (Australia), 250 Camberwell Road, Camberwell, Victoria 3124, Australia
(a division of Pearson Australia Group Pty. Ltd.)
Penguin Books India Pvt. Ltd., 11 Community Centre, Panchsheel Park, New Delhi—110 017, India
Penguin Group (NZ), 67 Apollo Drive, Rosedale, North Shore 0632, New Zealand
(a division of Pearson New Zealand Ltd.)
Penguin Books (South Africa) (Pty.) Ltd., 24 Sturdee Avenue, Rosebank, Johannesburg 2196,
South Africa
Penguin Books Ltd., Registered Offices: 80 Strand, London WC2R 0RL, England

While the author has made every effort to provide accurate telephone numbers and Internet addresses
at the time of publication, neither the publisher nor the author assumes any responsibility for errors,
or for changes that occur after publication. Further, the publisher does not have any control over and
does not assume any responsibility for author or third-party websites or their content.

TURKISH DELIGHT & TREASURE HUNTS

First American edition: September 2010
Portions of this book were originally published in Great Britain as *Cherry Cake and Ginger Beer*
(Hodder & Stoughton, 2008) and *Ripping Things to Do* (Hodder & Stoughton, 2009).

Perigee trade paperback ISBN: 978-0-399-53611-3

PRINTED IN THE UNITED STATES OF AMERICA

10   9   8   7   6   5   4   3   2   1

The recipes contained in this book are to be followed exactly as written. The publisher is not
responsible for your specific health or allergy needs that may require medical supervision. The
publisher is not responsible for any adverse reactions to the recipes contained in this book.

Most Perigee books are available at special quantity discounts for bulk purchases for sales promotions,
premiums, fund-raising, or educational use. Special books, or book excerpts, can also be created to fit
specific needs. For details, write: Special Markets, Penguin Group (USA) Inc., 375 Hudson Street, New
York, New York 10014.

# CONTENTS

# INTRODUCTION

**F**OR children the joy of reading books is twofold: First, there is the pleasure of being lost in a story, and second, there is the firing of the imagination that makes you want to do the things you have just been reading about. Who hasn't wanted to play croquet like Alice after reading *Alice's Adventures in Wonderland*? Or make gloriously inedible food mixtures like Betsy, Tacy, and Tib? Or create a time capsule like Tom and Petie in *The Midnight Fox*? Or eat a russet apple while reading a book in an attic like Jo in *Little Women*? Or host a tree party like Pippi Longstocking? Who has not, on reading a brilliant book, exclaimed, "I want to do that!"

This book is a collection of those "I want to do that!" moments. It's a book for adults who have never forgotten what it's like to read a great story and feel inspired to reenact it *immediately*, who can remember vividly what it was like to consume delicious food from the page and wish they could taste it for real. It's also for those who have perhaps forgotten but are happy to be reminded. And it's a book for anyone, young or old, who is looking for recipes for the food that children eat in books, as well as ideas for the best children's games and activities as played and invented by favorite literary characters. In addition, I hope that what you find between the covers of this book not only offer a starting point for many more cooking and creative adventures but will also encourage young readers to delve further into children's books because there is still plenty of buried treasure just waiting to be unearthed by avid readers.

*Turkish Delight and Treasure Hunts* is based on the wonderful foods and treats that children in books are forever enjoying and on the fantastic things they do when not eating, because it's a well-known truth that fictional children not only *eat* marvelous things, they also *do* all sorts of marvelous things. They enjoy amazing adventures, learn old-fashioned skills, invent wildly imaginative games, explore their world, and test themselves to the limit. They are full of ideas; they are busy, hungry, active, and resourceful, and they are a huge inspiration to readers who want so much to do and eat the things they do. They have delicious picnics, they create new dishes, and they know the value of a toasting fire and a good breakfast. They hunt for treasure, fly kites, and watch spiders spin webs.

Yet how many of us, when young or old, have copied Laura and her cousins in *Little House in the Big Woods* and flung hot maple syrup on snow to make hard candy, or eaten a mound of raspberry jam cakes at a Mary Poppins–style tea, or created a newspaper like the March girls? And how many would like to do such things, even if we can't quite re-create the special fictional surroundings in which we first encountered them? Quite a few, I'm sure.

But before we get carried away with ideas of exciting literary and culinary adventures, it must be pointed out that there are two types of activities in children's books: those that real children can do and those that real children can't do. As Alice in E. Nesbit's *Story of the Treasure Seekers* says with frustration, "You can't do half the things yourself that children in books do...I wonder why?" Alice recognizes, as do many young readers, that there is nothing worse than attempting to emulate your favorite character or being inspired by a brilliant book only to find the activity is impossible/suitable only for conquering heroes and explorers/costs a fortune/is highly dangerous/likely to be banned by adults/doesn't work. Though he may dream of experiencing for himself the freedom and independence enjoyed by characters in adventure books, the average child is generally unable to imitate the classic story device of absent parents; he can't get rid of his parents for a summer (or even completely) in order to be left on his own in the woods, up a tree, by a river, or in the kitchen. Nor can he normally obtain permission to go with siblings and friends on extended sailing and camping adventures without adults, or to leave home to seek treasure, all of which happens in many favorite, thrilling stories. No, I'm afraid there are some things that real boys and girls can't do, no matter how alluring or exciting the adventure, no matter how inventive, wily, or enterprising they are.

So this book plunders children's literature for all the wonderful things that they *can* do and make and eat. The idea behind it is to mine the classics for imaginative activities that are achievable, enjoyable, simple, thoughtful, manageable, and mostly pretty safe. (There are a few that carry an element of risk and for this I make no apology.)

When it came to food, I applied this practical criteria, and for an edible treat or specialty to qualify for inclusion, it had to be real food for humans and it had to be possible to make it in an ordinary home kitchen. There are many fabulous fantasy foods in books, but this is not the place for invented recipes that create dishes that no one has actually ever tasted in real life. So, no Harry Potteresque magic food, or Roald Dahl–style revolting recipes, I'm afraid. But as children's literature contains a feast, a *menu gastronomique*, of treats and lovely foodstuffs, there is no shortage of delights to choose from.

I adopted a similarly realistic approach to selecting which games and activities to include. So, as well as the gung-ho, challenging, adventurous, physical stuff that you would expect to find in a book of this nature, I have also included many more contemplative, thoughtful, creative things to do. This is because I think childhood is the time to acquire the habit of enjoying "small pleasantnesses," to borrow a phrase from Gwen Raverat's delightful childhood memoir *Period Piece*, and I like to think that this book could inspire children to learn poems by heart, pick ripe fruit from a tree, or make a rainbow with a prism, just as much as it might inspire boating, tree-climbing, and camping adventures.

So, where did I find these wonderful games and ideas? Well, I found them mostly in the classics, the books that have lasted longer than the generation for which they were written due to the fact that they have a timeless and universal appeal. The books I explored span a century or so, from the 1870s to the 1970s (a century that could be seen as "the golden age of children's literature"). I found it wasn't possible to go back much further than this because, even though I believe that children themselves have not changed, I found that childhood, or the way that childhood is presented by adult writers, has changed out of all recognition in a century and a half. Until the mid to late nineteenth century, books tended to be vehicles for improving, religious, and moral messages; amusement, imagination, and food were all secondary considerations, if they were considered at all. So, the period I cover begins with books by writers such as Louisa May Alcott, E. Nesbit, Frances Hodgson Burnett, and Susan Coolidge who were not afraid to include the delightful, everyday details of their characters' lives, which appealed directly to young readers (rather than their parents).

However, by the time we get to the early twentieth century, things are looking a lot more familiar, and we see the beginning of a new era of books written to entertain children and, even more daring, books that take a child's point of view. As a result, the books I cover are mostly from the twentieth century and are well-loved books in which children are children in a way we recognize and identify with, books that have influenced today's parents and grandparents so deeply.

The books from which I quote carry on up to the early 1970s with just the occasional more recent title included. This is not to say that there aren't many, many outstanding titles written after this date; it's just that the nature of the activities and foods in the books change around this time. Novels become grittier, more concerned with realism, and social and individual specific, and they begin to reflect the changes that take place in the home, the workplace, and the kitchen. With fewer mothers and

cooks making traditional cakes and cookies at home, food becomes faster, branded, more convenient, and the lavish teas and suppers enjoyed after nonstop adventuring, invented games, and traditional pastimes disappear as children's lives become more restricted and guarded.

And what did I leave out? Well, I deliberately excluded picture books in favor of books in which the printed word does the work in the child's imagination. I wanted to include games, activities, and edible treats whose appeal and resonance are created by the context in which they are discovered, and which are not simply inspired by an illustration, no matter how colorful, energetic, or mouthwatering.

When dealing with a series of books by a single writer, I have generally limited myself to the first title, for example, *Anne of Green Gables*, *A Bear Called Paddington*, and *Little Women*. To my mind, it's as if this first outing conveys the essence of the character in its best and purest form—like high-quality vanilla essence—so a small amount will give all the flavor you need. A secondary reason is that sequels often contain a foodstuff or an activity that is used as a recurring motif, like Paddington's marmalade sandwiches or the high-octane escapades in *Anne of Green Gables*.

Inevitably, though, some things had to be left out and some titles were omitted even though they fall into the correct time period and categories. Fantasy, science fiction, comic-strip books, most historical fiction, and stories about communities of animals are not covered because I had to draw the line somewhere, and although these genres often inspire many young readers' games, I decided to focus on "real" children in recognizable situations that could be emulated by children enthusiastic to try new foods, invent new pastimes, and learn news skills. It is for this reason that although I am passionate about many illustrated books and books for the very young, I chose not to include them and concentrated instead on longer reading books for older children because they contain so much more material and creative detail to act as springboards for the imagination.

Besides, the children in the books I cover have so much fun. I am fully aware that there are plenty more fictional characters who suffer and have unhappy, frightening experiences, and I would not for one minute deny the value of reading these, too, but as this book is a book of food and activities and not an exploration of character or circumstance, I have deliberately kept it positive, uplifting, quirky, amusing, entertaining, subversive, and very tasty.

The activities and foods that made it into the book are all ones that can be enjoyed by contemporary children; they were not chosen to be deliberately nostalgic. And even if they had been, I would make no excuses. Modern children are never short of books about children doing contemporary things and books that reflect the prevailing culture, but I think children need a mixed diet of influences and inspirations. They need to find out about the things children have always done, to make their own literary discoveries, and to expand their world and imagination, and not rely on dull-witted, boring parents who have forgotten what it's like to be a child. Adults often need reminding that children benefit enormously from a wide window on childhood, and not simply a mirror that reflects their own—and I firmly believe that books are the best way of providing this.

Jane Brocket
September 2010

# Amy's Pickled Limes

**F**OOD crazes in schools are nothing new, but they can be mystifying to those who weren't there at the time. However, the craze for pickled limes has passed into legend, thanks to Amy March's passion for them in *Little Women* (1868), and they have continued to intrigue many generations of readers. Indeed, Judy in *Daddy-Long-Legs* (1912) takes steps to discover what the fuss is about after finding it difficult to understand other students' references to pickled limes when she arrives at her new college:

> *I find I am the only girl in college who wasn't brought up on* Little Women. *I haven't told anybody though... I just went and bought it with $1.12 of my last month's allowance; and the next time somebody mentions pickled limes, I'll know what she's talking about.*

It's funny that this "contraband article," the pickled lime, still makes mouths water when mentioned in *Little Women*, and I particularly like the image of all those apparently sweet young ladies sucking on sour limes at their desks during lessons and then trading them for trinkets, favors, party invitations, and general popularity at recess. When Amy is undone by her lime-debts and lime-favors, it's as if this squeeze of lime juice is just what's needed to cut through the sugariness of her self-image and conceit, and the limes are used as a wonderfully tart metaphor.

Pickled limes sound so alluring and appetizing—particularly to contemporary readers who are currently in the middle of a fashion for sour sweets. Sourness holds a strange appeal for children, who have always loved treats such acid drops, lemon

1

sherbets, and sour plums with their underlying streak of acidity, which counteracts the sweetness and creates a daring flavor to excite youthful palates. It seems that pickled limes were simply an early forerunner of this slightly masochistic indulgence. Key limes, pickled in salt water and shipped from Florida to Boston, were a popular snack with schoolchildren on the East Coast of America in the mid-nineteenth century.

Taking my cue from the element of salt in the originals, I am giving this recipe for what I call Amy's Pickled Limes, but others may prefer to call them preserved limes. Today, the phrase *pickled limes* tends to mean a spicy condiment in which the limes are cooked with spices and oil, whereas preserved limes are similar to whole, preserved lemons that are prepared without any cooking and using just salt and juice.

MAKES 1 (16-OZ) JAR
*5–6 fresh, unblemished, unwaxed limes (enough to fill the jar when pressed down)*
*Fine salt*
*1 (16-oz) sealable jar, washed and sterilized*

1. Wash and dry the limes.

2. With a sharp knife, make four deep incisions from top to bottom in each lime. Take care not to cut right through the limes—they need to stay in one piece.

3. Pour a few tablespoons of salt into a bowl. Hold each lime over the bowl and gently press on the ends of the lime to open it up, one slit at a time. Press as much salt as you can into each slit and roll the lime in salt. Place in the jar.

4. Repeat the process for each lime and pack as many limes into the jar as possible.

5. Close the jar and shake well.

6. Leave for a week in a cool place. Shake the jar each day to disperse the liquid and salt. After the first week, store the limes in the fridge.

7. Eat, suck, or use in cooking.

# Run Your Own Post Office

Is it any wonder in these days of rapid, paperless, faceless, electronic communications that many children are still entranced by the idea of receiving old-fashioned letters in old-fashioned envelopes through the old-fashioned mailbox? My children are not above sending off for free samples just for the thrill of getting something addressed to them through the mail, and even their bank statements are opened with glee. When she was younger, my daughter Alice created her own little mailbox from a shoe box, and for quite some time her dad and I had to drop in a note or letter or card after she had gone to bed so that she had something to open in the morning. It wasn't difficult—more a matter of simply remembering, finding variations on our stationery, and thinking up little messages—but it was incredibly important to Alice.

This is why I think that many children would love to run their own little post office, something like the P.O. set up by Laurie and the March girls in Louisa May Alcott's *Little Women*, in an old bird box in the hedge that runs between their houses. It's big enough to hold "letters, manuscripts, books, and bundles" and each party has a key to the box. But it's the imaginative way in which it is used that makes it so appealing and such a great inspiration:

> *The P.O. was a capital little institution, and flourished wonderfully, for nearly as many queer things passed through it as through the real office. Tragedies and cravats, poetry and pickles, garden-seeds and long letters, music and ginger-bread, rubbers, invitations, scoldings and puppies. The old gentleman [Laurie's*

*grandfather] liked the fun, and amused himself by sending odd bundles, mysterious messages, and funny telegrams.*

In a foreshadowing of future uses and events, his gardener even sends a love letter to Hannah, the housekeeper, c/o Jo.

How could anyone give up on real mail after reading that?

### ❧ PRACTICAL ☙

Setting up a home post office is very straightforward, but it also has plenty of scope for development; once the participants are involved, they will no doubt come up with plenty of good ideas of their own.

#### SETTING UP A POST OFFICE

❦ A post office can be created anywhere in the house, apartment, or garden—a hedge is not essential. Use an old shoe box, or a larger box if you intend to post bigger items. Cut a rectangular hole, paint or spray-paint the box, or cover it with colored paper, and write on collection times, etc. If you plan to leave the post box outside it needs to be weather-, bird-, and squirrel-proof, with a lid that lifts and shuts tightly.

❦ It's very cheap and easy to make all you need from scratch, especially now that all types of documents and templates can be printed off computers. Older children can design their own documents, too.

❦ Design and make postage stamps on paper or light cardstock, or use stickers. Used stamps may come in handy (you'll need paper glue to restick them).

🕯 Buy date stamps and ink pads at stationery stores or look in craft shops for a wider range of stamps.

🕯 Collect brown paper, string, rubber bands, sticky labels, Scotch tape for parcels. Reuse large and padded envelopes.

🕯 Use kitchen scales for weighing letters and parcels, and a calculator for working out prices. Create postcards with photos or with images downloaded from the computer and printed on light cardstock. Recycle old cards, cut out pictures and illustrations, and use them to make "collage" cards.

🕯 Use plastic pretend money, Monopoly money, or set up your own bank and design and issue paper notes and coins. Or collect small change and foreign coins to use.

🕯 Visit a real post office for inspiration.

# Campfire Cocoa

❋

No matter how often it is drunk in literature, the mere mention of cocoa never fails to make everything better. Cocoa flows through hundreds of twentieth-century children's books—warming, comforting, cheering, hot, steaming, sweet, milky, always welcome, always delicious whether sipped under the stars or next to a fire, at a kitchen table or on a school bench, for breakfast, dinner, snack time, or supper. Books contain huge jugs of steaming cocoa, campfire cocoa, supper cocoa, caravan cocoa, cave cocoa, picnic cocoa, cocoa made with water, cocoa made with milk, cocoa sweetened with condensed milk or sugar, and cocoa enriched with a spoonful of cream.

Of all the cocoas I have come across, the one that stands out is the campfire cocoa in *The Secret of Spiggy Holes* by Enid Blyton. The children have everything they need for a perfect cocoa moment: a secret island, a dry night, soft heather, warm blankets and a rabbit-skin rug, a cheerful fire, kettle, and even a source of fresh spring water. Peggy is the cocoa expert and makes it with water and cocoa, adding canned, evaporated milk and sugar afterward, and it's enjoyed with cookies, tomato soup, bread, and a wonderful atmosphere. Cocoa, and life, don't get much better than this.

There's a vast difference between the indulgent, luxurious hot chocolate that is now in vogue, and the traditional, rather plain cocoa. Much as I like the occasional tiny cup of the former, I find cocoa far more drinkable and better suited to everyday occasions.

I'm giving two versions here; the first replicates the Spiggy Holes campfire cocoa made with canned, evaporated milk, and the second is a cocoa made with fresh milk. When we tested these, my daughter Phoebe and I were amazed at just how delicious steaming-hot cocoa can be, and the cocoa made with evaporated milk was a revelation.

## Campfire Cocoa I

**SERVES 6**
*1 tin good-quality cocoa powder*
*Boiling water*
*1 (14-oz) can evaporated milk*
*Sugar, to taste*

1. While the kettle is boiling, place 1½–2 teaspoons cocoa in each of 6 mugs.

**2.** Pour on the boiling water and stir well.

**3.** Add the milk and sugar, and serve immediately.

## Campfire Cocoa II

**MAKES 1 MUG**

*2 teaspoons sugar, or to taste*
*1 tablespoon good-quality cocoa powder*
*Enough milk to fill the mug (approximately 5–6 oz)*

**1.** Put the sugar and cocoa into a small pan with 2 tablespoons water. Heat gently and stir until smooth.

**2.** Allow the mix to boil for few seconds only, then slowly add the milk, stirring constantly.

**3.** Pour into the mug and serve very hot.

# Paddington Bear's Favorite Marmalade Buns

I know someone who used to say that he kept his morals in a suitcase under his bed. Well, Paddington Bear not only keeps his morals with him at all times, he also carries his suitcase wherever he goes, and always makes sure it contains a little something to eat in case of unplanned hunger.

Paddington is one in an illustrious line of hungry bears in children's literature, and many children are first introduced to marmalade by his passion for it. One of the joys of coming to London from Darkest Peru, where marmalade is scarce and regarded as a special treat, is that he is allowed by the generous and accommodating Brown family to have marmalade every day (and honey on Sundays). So Paddington Bear is able to buy his favorite marmalade buns with his pocket money, take marmalade sandwiches with him to the theater, and bring a jar of marmalade to the seaside.

While marmalade sandwiches may be too much of a good thing for younger palates, marmalade buns are more gently orangey. Here is a recipe for marmalade buns that would appeal to Paddington Bear. The kind of bun he might enjoy for "elevenses" with his good friend Mr. Gruber, who keeps an antique shop on Portobello Road in London:

*Mr. Gruber usually had a bun and a cup of cocoa in the morning for what he called "elevenses," and he had taken to sharing it with Paddington. "There's nothing like a chat over a bun and cocoa," he used to say, and Paddington, who liked all three, agreed with him—even though the cocoa did make his whiskers go a funny color.*

How wonderfully cozy-sounding and utterly irresistible.

The recipe below is very flexible and can be made as buns (small sponge cakes) or a single cake in a loaf pan. I ice my buns/cake with a simple icing made with confectioner's sugar and fresh orange juice, but they are also delicious without icing—and make far less mess in suitcases. They go just as well with tea, coffee, and orange juice as they do with cocoa, and it's worth reinstating elevenses simply as an excuse to eat them. They are also the perfect accompaniment to a reading-aloud session of favorite Paddington Bear stories.

### MAKES 1 LARGE CAKE OR 12 SMALL MUFFINS
*¾ cup (1½ sticks) butter*
*¾ cup light brown sugar*
*3 eggs*
*Grated zest of 1 orange (unwaxed)*
*Juice of ½ orange*
*2 rounded tablespoons thin-cut marmalade*
*¾ cups self-raising flour*

### FOR THE ICING:
*1½ cups confectioner's sugar*
*Juice of 1 orange*
*Orange food coloring (optional)*
*1 12-muffin pan and 12 paper liners, or 1 large (9 × 5-inch) loaf pan, greased with butter and lined with baking parchment*

1. Preheat the oven to 350°F. Line the muffin pan with paper liners, if using.

2. In a mixing bowl, beat the butter and sugar until light and fluffy. Add the eggs one by one until fully incorporated into the mix. Add the orange zest, orange juice, and marmalade, and stir in thoroughly.

3. Add the flour and fold in gently with a large metal spoon.

4. Divide the mix equally between the paper liners or spoon it into the loaf pan.

5. If you are making one cake, bake for 40–50 minutes, but check after 35 minutes. Use a metal skewer or sharp knife to test for doneness—insert it in the cake and if any trace of uncooked mixture comes out on the skewer or knife, the cake is not fully cooked. Return it to the oven and bake until the knife or skewer comes out clean. If you find your cake is browning a little too quickly, place a sheet of foil on top of the cake to prevent it from burning.

6. If you are making a dozen small muffins, they will need to bake for approximately 20 minutes.

7. Transfer the pan(s) to a wire rack and leave the muffins/cake to cool. Do not begin to ice them until they are completely cold.

8. To make the icing, sift the confectioner's sugar into a bowl and add half the orange juice and a tiny amount of orange food coloring, if using, and mix. Add as much juice as it takes to make the icing thick and glossy, and spread the icing over the muffins/cake.

# Master the Art of Breakfast in Bed

✳

Now this may sound indulgent, but I think everyone should be allowed the wizard, ripping, supersmashing treat of eating breakfast in bed from time to time.

I don't think the occasional room service is going to weaken morals or engender permanently lax attitudes to getting up, and I certainly don't think it should be only available to invalids. And anyway, everyone needs to master the art of eating breakfast in bed at some time in their life.

This is not as straightforward as you may think, as Paddington Bear discovers when Mrs. Bird comes into his room with a tray and announces that he's a "very privileged person to have breakfast in bed on a weekday!" (He certainly is.)

*It was the first time he had ever had breakfast in bed and he soon found it wasn't as easy as it looked. First of all he had trouble with the grapefruit. Every time he pressed it with his spoon a long stream of juice hit him in the eye, which was very painful.*

Meanwhile, the bacon and eggs are getting cold and the marmalade beckons.

*In the end he decided it would be much better if he mixed everything up on the one plate and sat on the tray to eat it.*

13

When Judy finds him a little while later he looks up with an "expression of bliss on his face; that part of his face which could be seen behind egg whiskers and toast crumbs."

Breakfast in bed *is* blissful, if a little messy. And plenty of early training in the art of preparing it will ensure that one day the trays are turned and the child who does this is the privileged person to whom it is delivered.

## WHAT YOU NEED FOR A
### PADDINGTON-STYLE BREAKFAST IN BED

- A tray that won't wobble

- A large napkin

- Plenty of toast, butter, jam, and a pot of the best marmalade

- Fried eggs and crispy bacon

- Mug of tea or coffee, or a glass of water, juice, or milk

- Half a grapefruit in a bowl and a spoon to gouge and press the fruit for maximum squirting

- A tissue or handkerchief to wipe the grapefruit juice from eyes

NOTE: Leftover bacon can be put in a suitcase and eaten later.

# Sara's Warming Currant Buns

❊

WITH its tale of Sara Crewe's journey from riches to rags and back again, *A Little Princess* by Frances Hodgson Burnett is an Edwardian Cinderella story with the exciting additions of a melodramatic plot, a heartless schoolmistress, snobby and sneaky schoolgirls, kind and generous heroes and heroines, cold garrets, hidden suffering, and overt moral messages. It's the kind of book that doesn't fade after reading, but continues to tug on the heartstrings for a lifetime.

After her father dies, poor Sara Crewe is shut out of the life to which she once belonged. She can only see the happy Large Family from the outside and catch glimpses of their cozy, warm, well-lit family life through the window of their house. She can only press her nose against the bright, delicious-smelling bakery and fantasize about eating warm currant buns, the epitome of all that is comforting and nourishing and all that's missing from her sad, lonely life as a servant at the Young Ladies' Seminary where she was once regarded as a little princess.

Then, one day, she finds a silver fourpenny piece in the gutter and, on looking up, she sees the baker's shop opposite where "a cheerful, stout, motherly woman with rosy cheeks was putting into the window a tray of delicious newly baked hot buns, fresh from the oven—large, plump, shiny buns, with currants in them." The shop is warm, the penny currant buns smell delicious, and the kind baker gives Sara six instead of four. But instead of eating all of them herself, she gives five to a beggar girl who is even hungrier and needier than she is. And it is then that we know, without a doubt, that Sara is a true princess.

Currant buns are one of the best known of all children's treats and appear regularly in books throughout the twentieth century. Characters rich and poor enjoy them fresh, stale, warm, cold, from paper bags or from pockets, at home, at school, for teas, picnics, or suppers, and always with gusto and satisfaction. They are sweetly and simply delicious, and deserve to be made in kitchens once again.

So here's a recipe for a classic currant bun to warm your body and soul. And to test the generosity and selflessness of any princess.

These currant buns could also be called sticky buns, that other staple of children's books. Made with or without the currants, they would pass muster with Snubby in Enid Blyton's Barney "R" Mysteries, who is a frequenter of "bun tents" (at events such as fairs and circuses), where sticky buns and lemonade are to be purchased and enjoyed.

MAKES 12 LARGE, PLUMP, SHINY BUNS

*¾ cup milk*
*2½ teaspoons active dry yeast*
*1 teaspoon runny honey or superfine sugar*
*5–5½ cups bread flour*
*¼ teaspoon see salt*
*¼ cup superfine sugar*
*¼ cup unsalted butter*
*2 eggs, beaten*
*Oil, for greasing*
*¾ cup currants*
*3 tablespoons superfine sugar*
*Jam and/or butter, to serve (optional)*
*Baking sheet, lined with baking parchment*

1. Warm the milk until it is lukewarm. It should not be too hot.

2. Put the yeast and honey or superfine sugar in a bowl, and add the milk. Stir well to mix. Leave to bubble while you prepare the rest of the ingredients. (If the mixture does not start to froth, this is because the yeast is no longer alive, and you will have to start again with new yeast.)

3. Put 5 cups of the flour and the salt and sugar in a large mixing bowl. Stir with your hand to mix the ingredients.

4. Add the butter and rub it into the dry ingredients until the mix resembles fine bread crumbs.

5. Pour in the milk and yeast mix, add the eggs, and mix well with one hand. If the mixture is too sticky to knead, add a little flour but not too much. This is a very well-behaved dough and will soon become manageable when you begin to knead it.

6. Turn the dough out onto a floured work surface and knead gently for 5–7 minutes until it becomes elastic and smooth. Form into a ball.

7. Lightly grease the mixing bowl with oil. Return the dough to the bowl, cover with plastic wrap, and leave to rise in a warm spot for 2–3 hours, until it has doubled in size.

8. Preheat the oven to 400°F.

9. Punch down the dough (deflate it with a floured hand) and turn it onto a floured work surface. Sprinkle the currants over the dough and knead gently to incorporate them.

10. Weigh the dough and divide it into twelve equal pieces. Roll each piece into a ball and place on the baking sheet,

close together but not touching. Cover with plastic wrap and leave to rise for 30–45 minutes.

11. Bake for 20 minutes until the buns are golden brown and sound hollow when tapped on the base. Toward the end of baking, make the glaze by bringing the superfine sugar and 3 tablespoons water to boiling point in a small pan.

12. Remove the tray from the oven and put on a wire rack. Brush the buns immediately with the glaze.

13. These buns are wonderful when warm. Eat as they are or with jam and/or butter.

# Secret Gardening

IN some ways, flower bulbs are even more magical than seeds. They are like buried treasure: Simply hide them in the earth in autumn, leave them to get on with their secret underground

life, and you are rewarded in spring with the most glorious flowers.

Mary in *The Secret Garden* by Frances Hodgson Burnett realizes something wonderful is happening under the soil when she first explores the hidden garden in early spring. She finds little green shoots in the overgrown grass and weeds, and gently clears spaces for them to "breathe" and grow. As the weather gets warmer, they become stunning snowdrops and daffodils, and clumps of orange, purple, and gold crocuses that delight Mary so much she feels compeled to kiss them.

But then, bulbs do this to some people, and although not everyone is moved to kiss crocuses, there is nothing to match the joy of watching the shoots and flowers emerge from the earth after a hard winter, in a burst of color and fragrance.

### ◆ PRACTICAL ◆

Bulbs are an excellent way of starting children off with simple gardening. They need nothing more than a bag of bulbs, a patch of soil or a pot or two of compost, and a trowel (or even an old spoon) for digging little holes. They also enjoy writing the labels to put in the soil so that they can be reminded of what is growing where.

- Daffodils are the easiest bulbs to grow. They are unfussy and reappear and multiply year after year. Plant in September.

- Crocuses are also very straightforward and should be planted in September. They, too, reappear each spring.

- Tulips are a little fussier and most varieties don't make repeat performances after the first year. On the other hand, the flowers are stunning and the colors amazing. Plant in November.

🌱 If I had to choose one beginners' bulb, it would be the hyacinth. The bulbs can be planted outside in September, but you can also buy "prepared" bulbs for growing indoors later in the year (November/December). This means children can watch their progress even more closely, especially if the bulbs are grown in the specially designed hyacinth vases that are available from garden centers and supermarkets (often with a single bulb as part of a boxed gift set) in late autumn and the run-up to Christmas. Simply place the bulb in the neck of the vase, fill with water to just below but not touching the bulb, and in no time at all the vase will be filled with a swirling mass of white roots. It's not long before a thick, green shoot appears, which eventually produces a stem with masses of sweetly scented flowers.

🌱 Hyacinths are worth growing for their fragrance alone. It pervades *Tom's Midnight Garden* by Philippa Pearce: For Tom, who is sent away from home to avoid measles, the hyacinths in the flower beds in the garden are powerfully evocative and their smell reminds him of his mother's indoor bulb pots at Christmas and New Year. They are the flowers he knows best, the ones whose scent convinces him that the garden must be real.

🌱 A lovely secret garden effect can be created with masses of bulbs—buy them in bulk at much lower prices from bulb wholesalers.

# Dickon's Roasted Eggs

ONE of the joys of reading *The Secret Garden* is devouring the large number of taste-bud-tingling descriptions of food eaten outdoors. Although it is fresh, plain, and simple, it always sounds wonderful in this context. How about: "roasted eggs and potatoes and richly frothed new milk and oat-cakes and buns and heather honey and clotted cream."

All these food moments mean that, as sure as "eggs is eggs," whenever I read *The Secret Garden* I have an urge to make roasted eggs. Although in Britain we have had roast beef, roast potatoes, and roast chestnuts for centuries, and have recently embraced the more exotic roast peppers, figs, and squash, somewhere along the way we lost the art of roasting eggs.

Roasted eggs have a very distinct appeal; it's as though the action of placing them in the glowing embers of a fire confers a certain hitherto-unknown cachet on the humble egg. And indeed, they make the perfect outdoor food, cooking gently while children run around and play and work up an appetite.

In *The Secret Garden*, roasted eggs are a symbolic part of the diet that brings both Mary and Colin back to life and health. Dickon discovers

> a deep little hollow where you could build a sort of tiny oven with stones and roast potatoes and eggs in it. Roasted eggs were a previously unknown luxury, and very hot potatoes with salt and fresh butter in them were fit for a woodland king—besides being deliciously satisfying.

Although you may wonder how it is that they don't crack or explode, I can assure you they do work.

**1–2 EGGS PER PERSON**
*Baked potatoes, salt, butter, and fresh milk, to serve*

1. If you have a needle or something sharp on hand, make a tiny hole in the shell at one end of each egg.
2. Hold the egg under a tap or immerse it in water to wet the outside.
3. Place in the embers of a fire or in a cool (300°F) oven.
4. Cook for 1 hour.
5. Leave to cool for a few minutes before peeling.
6. Serve with potatoes baked in the fire or oven, salt, butter, and fresh milk.

# Skipping School

*

Ageneration ago, jump ropes were the preserve of girls in playgrounds, happily chanting counting rhymes, jumping rhythmically up and down, and running around with a rope whooshing overhead and underfoot. There may have been the occasional glimpse on television of a boxer skipping manically to lose weight before a weigh-in, but that was about it. Nowadays, however, the jump rope seems to have vanished from the children's playground and into the adults' gym, so it's high time it was brought back. After all, as Martha's mother says in *The Secret Garden* by Francis Hodgson Burnett, a skipping rope is "the sensiblist toy a child can have."

She sends a skipping rope via Martha to the pale, weak, and sad Mary, who has no idea what it is. Martha demonstrates how to skip indoors and Mary's interest is aroused. Off she goes, into the fresh air, to begin building up her puny arms and legs.

*The skipping-rope was a wonderful thing. She counted and skipped, and skipped and counted, until her cheeks were quite red.*

Mary skips hither and thither, enjoying the wind and the outdoor scents, skipping around the fountain and into the kitchen garden, setting herself little challenges and laughing with pleasure until she skips right up to the robin who shows her the door to the secret garden.

Indeed, jumping rope unlocks the child in Mary at the same time that the key unlocks the door to the secret garden, and both are saved.

## ❧ PRACTICAL ❧

Jumping rope is cheap and easy, and still one of the best forms of energetic play for boys and girls.

- 🏵 You can buy jump ropes from toy stores or online, or alternatively children can use a length of rope or washing line.

- 🏵 Jumping rope can be done by individual jumpers or by groups jumping over a longer rope that is held and turned by two players, one at each end.

- 🏵 Revisit the jumping rhymes, games, and tricks of your childhood and pass them on.

### JUMPING RHYMES

🏵 A rhyme to accompany the jumper jumping over the rope as many times as possible without missing:

Mabel, Mabel, set the table,
Just as fast as you are able.
[Don't forget the salt, mustard, vinegar, pepper] (*repeat faster and faster until the jumper is out*)

🏵 A rhyme for swinging the rope back and forth, and then over the jumper:

Blue bells, cockle shells,
Easy ivy over

🏵 Rhymes that call in friends to jump together or take turns:

Rooms for rent, inquire within,
As I move out, let (*name*) come in.
I love coffee, I love tea.
I want (*name*) to come in with me.

I had a little puppy
His name was Tiny Tim
I put him in the bathtub, to see if he could swim
He drank up all the water, he ate up all the soap
The next thing you know he had a bubble in his throat.
In came the doctor (*person jumps in*)
In came the nurse (*person jumps in*)
In came the lady with the alligator purse (*person
    jumps in*)
Out went the doctor (*person jumps out*)
Out went the nurse (*person jumps out*)
Out went the lady with the alligator purse (*person
    jumps out*)

❦ A rhyme for jumping then running around one of the people turning the rope before rejoining:

I had a little bumper car,
Number 48,
Whizzed round the corner...
(*the jumper leaves the skipping and runs around one of the
    rope turners while everyone says "corner," then rejoins the
    jumping*)
Slams on the brakes

# Make a Time Capsule

TIME capsules are a sort of personal message in a bottle that you can actually rely on finding again. And although the public or school-organized time capsules are worthy and well meaning, they can never be as interesting as an individual time capsule put together for its maker's future interest. This is the type of capsule made by Tom and Petie in *The Midnight Fox*, the excellent coming-of-age-during-the-course-of-one-summer novel by Betsy Byars.

The story, and the time capsule within it, both emphasize how quickly children alter and how they can become almost unrecognizable to themselves year after year. At the end of the summer of change, Tom looks back and realizes that "it all seemed like something that had happened to another boy instead of me. Like the time Petie and I made a time capsule out of a large jar, and we put into this jar all kinds of things, so that in a hundred years, or a thousand, someone would find this capsule, open it, and know exactly what Petie Burkis and I had been like."

As it is, they don't leave their capsule to posterity but dig it up themselves after a year and, when they look at the contents,

*Petie kept saying "I never wrote that. I know I never wrote that"…*
*it was as if two other boys had made up the time capsule and buried*
*it in the ground.*

The boys had put in pictures of themselves and lists of things they had done, stories they had written about their families for English lessons, pictures, and a poem. Petie wrote

27

down everything he'd eaten and drunk in one day, and Tom wrote down all the books he had read in the last year. It's all intensely personal and meaningful and, for the boys, a quite amazing archaeological find even after just twelve months.

## ❧ PRACTICAL ❧

🎋 A time capsule can be a one-off or it can be part of an Andy Warhol–style series (between 1974 and 1987 he made more than six hundred cardboard-box time capsules full of now valuable ephemera). For example, there could be one for every summer of a child's life, or each New Year's Day.

### SUGGESTIONS FOR TIME CAPSULES

🎋 If you plan to bury the time capsule, make sure it is watertight, waterproof, and nonbiodegradable, for example, made out of tin or plastic or glass. Use a cookie sheet or cake pan and seal well, a clip-and-seal food container, or a large glass jar.

🎋 Draw up a map to show the whereabouts of the capsule so that it can be easily located when it's time to dig it up.

🎋 Alternatively, box up your items in a cardboard box, seal and label it, and ask someone to hide it for you. Make sure they make a note of the hiding spot.

🎋 Put in details of the name of the maker, the date of making, and fill with things that represent you at that moment, for a composite snapshot of who you are.

🎋 Further suggestions include photos of family, friends and pets, lists, theater or sports programs, newspaper headlines, examples of favorite toys, current photos, CDs of photos, or homemade films.

🏆 Agree on a digging-up or opening date. No peeking in advance!

# Play Croquet Like Alice

*Alice soon came to the conclusion that it was a very difficult game indeed.*

Well, when you are knocking hedgehogs (instead of balls) with flamingos (instead of mallets) through bent-over playing cards (instead of hoops), I think anyone would find croquet difficult.

Croquet has a reputation for being a little mad (and the surreal situation Alice finds herself in is madder than ever), but maybe this is why it fascinates children. Perhaps the fact that most households do not possess a perfectly smooth, flat lawn or a set of heavy wooden mallets, leather balls, and metal hoops makes them realize that croquet is the sort of game that invites all sorts of fantastic improvisations.

Read Lewis Carroll's *Alice's Adventures in Wonderland* with them and they'll immediately seek out walking sticks and umbrellas, find or make a sphere to act as a ball, and use legs or books to create arches. Then they are away, shouting "Off with her head!" and turning into imperious duchesses with one swing of their "mallets."

## ⊷ PRACTICAL ⊷

If you are curious to learn the rules of the real game, go to www .toycrossing.com/croquet/play.shtml, but children are brilliant at taking the concept of croquet and altering it to suit their situations and whims.

🌱 Surreal croquet works well indoors if soft balls are used and propelled along the floor (not played golf style).

🎯 If children want to play proper croquet outside, the U.S. Croquet Association at www.croquetamerica.com sells children's and junior croquet sets, as do other websites.

🎯 One of the most memorable improvised games we have played was literary table tennis in a vacation house. The large dining table was cleared, a line of hardback books placed spine up across the middle for a net, and each player chose a small, hardback book as a bat. The only concession to real table tennis was a proper Ping-Pong ball. This setup worked surprisingly well.

# Katy's Paradise Picnic Pie

IT's funny how children can often miss the morals in so many well-meaning books. *What Katy Did* by Susan Coolidge made a huge impression on me, but I'm afraid its *Pilgrim's Progress* moral went right over my head. I was too busy reliving in my imagination Katy's terrible accident and rooting for her recovery to realize just how tamed and *improved* she had become. (And wondering why so many characters in late Victorian literature broke their backs, like Katy, or their legs, and/or were confined to wheelchairs and beds.)

I was also sidetracked by the food. Long before the real drama happens, Katy and her brothers and sisters go to the place they call "Paradise" for a never-to-be-repeated summer picnic. "Paradise" is a marshy thicket beyond the symbolic gate (no doubt modeled on the "Wicket Gate" in *Pilgrim's Progress*) where the children decorate a tiny and very private "bower" or den, just large enough for them, their two food baskets, and their kitten. The afternoon turns into one of pure, unadulterated childish happiness:

> *First came a great many ginger cakes…buttered biscuit came next—three apiece, with slices of cold ham laid in between; and last of all were a dozen hard-boiled eggs, and a layer of thick bread and butter sandwiched with corned beef…Oh, how good everything tasted in that bower…no grown-up dinner-party ever had so much fun.*

And it doesn't stop there because this really is paradise, so there must be some paradise pies:

*…and there—oh, delightful surprise—were seven little pies— molasses pies, baked in saucers—each with a brown top and crisp, candied edge, which tasted like toffee and lemon-peel, and all sorts of good things mixed up together. There was a general shout…a tumult of joy…in an incredibly short time every vestige of pie had disappeared, and a blissful stickiness pervaded the party.*

In their "blissful stickiness," the children discuss what they want to do with their lives, and Katy describes the many ways in which she will be "an ornament to the family." It's a perfect, crystallized moment and, as it turns out, the awful pride before her fall.

The description of those molasses pies lingers on the taste buds of the imagination long after the picnic, long after Katy's swing breaks, long after her suffering and redemption. The pies embody the sweetness and mix of good things in this idyllic picnic; they are most definitely celebratory rather than improving and are definitely worth preserving and making.

Since molasses does not play a huge part in British baking, I've decided to adapt the treat slightly to make a "paradise pie" and have used dark brown sugar (available in supermarkets) and lemon peel to make a paradise version of the classic American sugar pie. This recipe makes one large pie, but it would work well as smaller pies baked in individual pie pans. I make the pastry by hand as I don't have a food processor.

MAKES 1 PIE (SERVES 8)
1¾ cups all-purpose flour
1 tablespoon confectioner's sugar
6 tablespoons cold butter
Grated zest of 1 lemon (unwaxed), plus lemon juice to mix
    (optional)
1 egg yolk

FOR THE FILLING:
1 cup soft dark brown sugar
1 lemon (unwaxed)
⅓ cup all-purpose flour
Pinch salt
1¼ cups–1¾ cups heavy cream
Nutmeg, to grate
8.5-inch tart or pie tin, greased with butter

1. Sift the flour and confectioner's sugar into a large bowl. Add the butter and rub it in until the mix resembles fine bread crumbs.

2. Stir in the lemon zest, then add the egg yolk and 2 teaspoons lemon juice or water. Mix with a knife or your hand, adding tiny amounts of liquid as necessary to bring the dough together into a ball. Add as little liquid as possible.

3. Shape the dough into a disk, cover it in plastic wrap, and chill it in the fridge for 30 minutes, or until you are ready to use it.

4. Preheat the oven to 350°F.

5. Roll the dough out on a floured surface and carefully line the tin with it; make sure you cover the sides of the tin right up to the top edge as the pastry will shrink a little during baking. Prick the base a few times with a fork, cover the whole case with foil, and place a layer of dried beans on the base (to stop the pastry from rising up).

6. Bake for 15 minutes. Remove the beans and foil, then return the pastry to the oven to bake for another 5 minutes or until it is pale gold and dry. Remove from oven and let cool slightly.

7. Meanwhile, to make the filling, put the sugar in a mixing bowl and grate the zest of the lemon over it.

8. Sift in the flour and salt. Mix with a fork or your fingers, breaking up any lumps in the sugar until you have a fine, crumbly mix.

9. When the pastry shell is cooked, tip in the filling mix and spread it evenly over the base.

10. Measure out 1¼ cups of the cream in a glass measuring cup and warm it slightly.

11. Pour the cream over the filling mix until the pastry case is almost but not quite full. Add more cream if necessary to bring it to the correct level.

12. Bake for 35–45 minutes, until the surface starts to turn brown. Remove and leave to cool on a wire rack. The filling will initially appear quite runny, but it will set as the pie cools.

# Enjoy a Weekend Retreat

WEEKEND retreats should not be just the province of stressed-out adults—children need their space, too. And if they are allowed to retreat, well then, the adults get more space, too. Children don't need to disappear too far away but can be safe and happy close by in places like attics, lofts, sheds, and barns.

In *What Katy Did* by Susan Coolidge, Katy, her siblings, and her best friend, Cecy Hall, often retreat en masse to various favorite, private places, and their aunt Izzy can't understand their "queer notions about getting off into holes and corners and poke-away places." On rainy Saturday afternoons they head off to the loft to enjoy a "splendiferous" feast with stories, verses, performances, and the ceremonial passing around of a bottle of vinegar and water. They eat delicious-sounding caraway cookies with scalloped edges and suck sticks of cinnamon; it makes something very ordinary—a group of children in a loft—appear quite marvelous and provides a charming idea to copy.

Katy and the others are not the only ones who escape from family life to a private space. Books contain lots of children who are happily ensconced and perched up high in lofts and attics, surrounded by the discarded and stored jumble and treasures of the house.

Pollyanna's retreat is her attic bedroom, Jo in Louisa May Alcott's *Little Women* loves nothing more than reading and writing and eating apples in her garret room, and the Railway Children hold their "councils" in the loft. Sara Crewe's attic bedroom in *A Little Princess* by Frances Hodgson Burnett is at first a bare and lonely place, but in time it becomes a place of refuge, comfort, companionship, and hot tea and muffins. Another weekend retreat is the ham and pepper and onion–filled, spicy-smelling attic in Laura Ingalls Wilder's *Little House in the Big Woods*, where Laura and Mary go to play in winter: "Often the wind howled outside with a cold and lonesome sound. But in the attic Laura and Mary played house with the squashes and pumpkins and everything was snug and cozy." And Jo Ruggles in *The Family from One End Street* by Eve Garnett reminds us of one of the best weekend retreats of all: the movie theater, where you can, like him, indulge in hours of fantasy and escapism on a Saturday afternoon.

### IDEAS FOR A WEEKEND RETREAT

A loft, attic, or garret is not essential. Retreats can be taken in spare rooms, in indoor and outdoor dens, in tents and any "hole," "corner," or "poke-away place." The following are suggestions for what to do:

- Form a club
- Tell stories
- Write a play
- Dress up and put on a show
- Practice magic tricks
- Tell fortunes
- Learn new codes
- Set up a detective agency

- 🌵 Write a newspaper

- 🌵 Eat homemade cookies

- 🌵 Go to see a film. Many movie theaters still have children's weekend matinees with vastly reduced ticket prices, so it's worth checking in advance.

# Debby's Jumbles

❋

*[Katy] could wait no longer, but crept out of bed, crossed the floor on tiptoe, and raising the lid [of the box] a little put in her hand. Something crumby and sugary met it, and when she drew it out, there, fitting on her finger like a ring, was a round cake with a hole in the middle of it.*

*"Oh! it's one of Debby's jumbles!" she exclaimed.*

When I mentioned on my blog, Yarnstorm, that I was writing this book, I had an amazing response from readers who went into raptures about their own favorite books and treats. One treat in particular stood out by dint of it being so well known and yet still a mystery. What exactly are jumbles, the treats that Katy and her sister Clover eat on Christmas morning in *What Katy Did at School*?

Jumbles were popular in England and other European countries during the seventeenth and eighteenth centuries when they were also known as *gemmels* from the German word for twin, and were so called because they were originally in the shape of two entwined rings. In the nineteenth century, they were taken to America where, according to a recipe printed in 1855, they became less hard, more spongy, and circular. A recipe in an American cookbook of 1917 suggests that by then they were softer and thinner and more like sugar cookies, and the central hole had to be cut out with a cutter. Back in England, they eventually turned into flat, crisp, waferlike thins to be served with desserts (as mentioned by Agnes Jekyll who gives a recipe for orange jumbles in *Kitchen Essays*, written in 1922).

But Debby's jumbles are of the ring variety, so that is what this recipe makes. Debby is clearly an accomplished cook (her muffins are light and her clear crab-apple jelly comes out of the mold perfectly) and her jumbles are a wonderful taste of home for Katy and Clover, who jump excitedly back into bed, to nibble and chatter on Christmas morning.

Jumbles can be flavored with lemon zest (as in this recipe) or with orange zest, caraway seeds, almond essence, rosewater, or brandy. Just add a few drops of flavoring liquid, half a teaspoon of seeds, or grated zest to the basic recipe.

MAKES 12–15 JUMBLES, OR ENOUGH FOR A GIRL TO WEAR RINGS ON HER FINGERS *AND* A FEW RINGS ON HER TOES
*½ cup (1 stick) butter, softened*
*¾ cup superfine sugar, plus extra for sprinkling*
*2 eggs*
*Grated zest of 1 lemon (unwaxed)*
*2¾ cups self-raising flour*
*Milk, for brushing*
*Baking sheet, lined with baking parchment*

1. Preheat the oven to 350°F.
2. In a mixing bowl, cream the butter and sugar until pale and fluffy.
3. Beat in the eggs one at a time.
4. Add the lemon zest and sift in the flour and gently fold into the mixture with a metal spoon.
5. Divide the mixture into 12–15 pieces, roll them out into sausages approximately 6 inches long, and form them into rings. Make sure the holes in the middle are quite large, as the mixture will spread during baking and you don't want

them to close up. Place well apart on the baking sheet, brush with milk, and sprinkle generously with superfine sugar.

6. Bake for 15–20 minutes until pale golden. Leave the jumbles to cool before wearing and/or eating.

# Make Danny's Marvelous Father's Marvelous Toad-in-the-Hole

*"Dad, would you be able to make your favorite thing of all?"*
*"What's that?" he asked.*
*"Toad-in-the-hole," I said.*
*"By golly!" he cried. "That'll be the very first thing we'll make in our new oven! Toad-in-the-hole! I'll make it in an enormous pan, same as my old mum, with the Yorkshire pudding very crisp and raised up in huge bubbly mountains and the sausages nestling in between the mountains!"*

*Danny the Champion of the World* is Roald Dahl's wonderful, heartwarming tale of a widowed father and his only son who are united against the world by a deep bond of love and affection. They live a bohemian life in a gypsy caravan, eat windfall apples, cook a very limited range of dishes on a single paraffin burner, and are idyllically happy until outside agencies and busybodies start to interfere.

By the end of the tale, though, Danny's father realizes it's time they had a proper oven in which to roast food such as pork and lamb and beef and, of course, pheasant. But it is the much homelier comfort food—toad-in-the-hole—that they decide to make first, a dish that brings back memories of warm kitchens and a mother's home cooking.

Toad-in-the-hole is probably the ultimate in male-bonding food; it's a laughably, self-consciously macho dish that depends for full effect on pantomimic proportions of whopping sausages and magically rising batter. It has everything needed to please and entertain and satisfy anyone with a boyish sense of humor and is a great recipe for dads and boys (or, indeed, any other family combination) to make together. And it's clearly just the thing for a great vacation.

## ❧ PRACTICAL ❧

This is the recipe we use, and it gives a generous ratio of batter to sausage. It uses comically fat pork sausages, but you can use whatever type of sausage you prefer. And as for the gravy, well, I would guess that Danny and his marvelous dad wouldn't turn their noses up at instant gravy in their gypsy caravan, but homemade onion gravy is very delicious if you have the time and inclination to make it.

## Toad-in-the-Hole

SERVES 6
*3½ cups plain flour*
*½ teaspoon salt*
*3 eggs*
*3¾ cups milk*
*2–3 sausages per person (or according to taste and appetite)*
*2 tablespoons beef drippings or lard for frying the sausages (or*
   *3–4 tablespoons mild olive oil or vegetable oil)*
*1 large roasting pan or 2 smaller pans*

1. Preheat the oven to 425°F.

2. First make the batter: Sift the flour and salt into a large mixing bowl. Make a well in the center and crack the eggs into it. Beat with a whisk, gradually incorporating the milk until you have a smooth liquid. Leave to stand while you get the sausages ready.

3. Heat half the fat or oil in a large frying pan and brown the sausages for 5 minutes. Remove the sausages with a slotted spoon and put on a plate until needed.

4. Pour the leftover hot fat or oil into the roasting pan(s), add the rest of the fat or oil, and heat in the oven for a few minutes until smoking hot.

5. Remove the pan(s) from the oven, pour in the batter, and arrange the sausages in the batter.

6. Return the pan(s) to the oven and cook until puffed up and browned. This will take 30–35 minutes for the smaller pans and up to 45 minutes for the large pan.

7. Serve immediately with gravy.

# Pick Your Own Fruit

*It is the most marvelous thing to be able to go out and help yourself to your own apples whenever you feel like it. You can do this only in the autumn of course, when the fruit is ripe, but all the same, how many families are so lucky?... Our apples were called Cox's Orange Pippins, and I liked the sound of the name almost as much as I liked the apples.*

In Roald Dahl's *Danny the Champion of the World*, Danny has an interesting, cash-strapped, bohemian lifestyle with his widowed but very marvelous dad, and he fully appreciates and enjoys the fact that he can simply stretch out and pick a deliciously ripe piece of fruit straight from a tree above their gypsy caravan. In many ways, what Danny has is the ultimate pick-your-own experience.

It's ironic that this type of fruit-picking experience has become something of a luxury or a special treat for many children these days. Which is a shame, because picking ripe fruit is something very special, something absolutely of a perfect summer moment, and something every child, ordinary or bohemian, should experience.

## ✌ PRACTICAL ✌

There are several ways of picking your own fruit: grow it, pick it for free from friends' or neighbors' trees, or go to a "pick-your-own" farm.

🌱 Older neighbors, friends, and family members may be happy to let children pick fruit rather than see it go to waste, if they are unable to pick it themselves or need help doing so.

🌱 There are now many pick-your-own farms in the United States; search the Internet for "pick your own farms" to find one near you. It's a great family activity and the freshly picked fruit always tastes extra delicious.

🌱 Alternatively, just one or two fruit trees in a garden can provide enough pickings for a family, and allow for the luxury of eating ripe fruit straight from their branches. Choose fruits that everyone likes, such as plums, apples, or pears.

🌱 Even if you are short on space, it's possible to grow small bushes of fruit like red currants, black currants, and gooseberries in pots. Strawberries are particularly good for growing in pots and window boxes because the fruit can hang over the sides to ripen without the risk of being eaten by slugs or affected by rot—and children love picking the ripe ones as they appear.

### GROWING STRAWBERRIES IN POTS

🌱 Buy strawberry plants from garden centers in mid-spring or raise from seed, if you prefer, and plant in 10-inch-wide plant pots (terra cotta looks nice, but plastic works just as well).

🌱 Put a layer of gravel or broken crocks in the base of each pot, then fill the pot with multipurpose potting compost.

🌱 Make a hole for the strawberry plant, which should sit level with the surface of the compost (not above it), and water in well.

❧ Keep the strawberry pots in a light, sunny position and water frequently, especially in dry spells. Pick the strawberries as they ripen.

❧ Discard the plants after a maximum of four years.

# *Fly a Kite*

**✳**

**D**ADS are brilliant. But it's often the clever, quirky little things they do rather than any grand gestures or paternal heroics that remain in the memory. Danny's dad in Roald Dahl's *Danny the Champion of the World* is exactly the kind of father who possesses all sorts of marvelous, useful, and exciting skills.

"My father, without the slightest doubt, was the most marvelous and exciting father any boy ever had."

He's the dad of your dreams. He can mend cars, catch pheasants, make fire balloons, tree houses, bows and arrows, stilts, whizzers, and boomerangs—and as he and Danny live a pretty bohemian life, the two of them can also be wonderfully spontaneous. If there's a wind, why not make a kite and fly it?

*"There's a good wind today," he said one Saturday morning. "Just right for flying a kite. Let's make a kite, Danny."*

*So we made a kite.*

Kite making is one of those skills that is in danger of dying out. These days, there are fewer and fewer fathers, uncles, and big brothers who know how to make a kite from a few pieces of wood, an old shirt, and some string, and young boys (and girls) are missing out on the magic of flying a homemade kite. So watch carefully now as Danny's father demonstrates:

*He showed me how to splice four thin sticks together in the shape of a star, with two more sticks across the middle to brace it. Then we cut up an old blue shirt of his and stretched the material across the framework of the kite. We added a long tail made of thread, with*

*little leftover pieces of the shirt tied at intervals along it...and he showed me how to attach the string to the frame-work so that the kite would be properly balanced in flight.*

Danny is amazed and thrilled that the kite flies successfully, rising up and bobbing for hours on the wind. Not every dad can make a kite, but every dad (or big brother/granddad/uncle) can have a go at flying one.

### ❧ PRACTICAL ☙

🎗 There are plenty of books with good instructions for making kites, but various woodworking and manual skills are required, which may defeat some potential kite makers. Also, and I do not want to dampen anyone's enthusiasm, there is nothing more disappointing than a kite made with high hopes that simply refuses to fly. So there is a good argument for buying a basic kite and learning how to fly it before attempting to make one. There is no use making everyone miserable by hammering and splicing and bracing, then finding the result won't get off the ground.

🎗 There is just as much fun in taking a store-bought kite and climbing a hill or going to a deserted park, field, or beach on a blustery day, and watching your kite rise and bob and pull on the string. Young boys and girls will still think you are "marvelous" for flying kites with them.

🎗 Alternatively, the fun might be in making a kite of your own design, and messing about with sticks and shirts and string. As long as you remember to laugh if it (and your hopes) falls to earth with a crash. On the other hand, though, it may soar like Danny's.

# Bruce Bogtrotter's Heroic
# Chocolate Cake

CHILDREN'S books have their fair share of unappetizing, large children who are used by their creators to make statements about greed and rudeness and self-control (or lack thereof), and Roald Dahl's books contain an exceptionally high number of dire warnings. So it's not often that overeating is seen as a heroic, self-determining act, and this makes Bruce Bogtrotter's cake-eating feat in *Matilda* all the more impressive.

Although Dahl himself loved chocolate, he ate it in moderation and clearly disliked overindulgence. But eating in order to defy a nasty, bullying teacher is of a different order of chocolate eating, and in this brilliant scene Dahl exploits the one area of control that children can exercise over adults—whether or not to accept or refuse food, or, as in this case, eat something in order to make a glorious statement of independence.

Bruce Bogtrotter is a cake thief and has stolen a slice of the chocolate cake belonging to the terrifying, bullying teacher, the Trunchbull, and his punishment is to be made to eat a huge, humiliating cake in front of the school. But Bruce Bogtrotter rises to the challenge and, far from melting away, his confidence grows with each slice until the children sense that he is winning an enormous battle with the Trunchbull. Finally, by dint of sheer willpower, cheered on by the children, he triumphs by eating the entire cake.

Not long ago, my daughter Phoebe made an incredibly large, rich, and filling chocolate cake for a birthday, and it occurred to me that this was exactly the kind of cake that Bruce Bogtrotter could eat on his own if pressed to defend himself. None of us could eat more than a slice or so—not even my son Tom's hungry teenage friends who declared it the best chocolate cake they'd ever tasted—and it was then that I understood just how brave Bruce Bogtrotter had been. So here is Phoebe's recipe for a heroic chocolate cake.

**MAKES 1 VERY LARGE CAKE (SERVES 12–16)**
1¾ cups soft light brown sugar
1½ cups (3 sticks) unsalted butter, softened
6 eggs
2¾ cups self-raising flour
¾ cup good-quality cocoa powder
1 teaspoon baking powder
2–3 tablespoons milk
Chocolate buttons, to decorate (optional)

**FOR THE FILLING AND TOPPING:**
1¾ cups confectioner's sugar
1 cup good-quality cocoa powder
⅔ cup unsalted butter, softened
3–4 tablespoons milk
10-inch round cake pan, greased with butter and lined with
    baking parchment

1. Preheat the oven to 350°F.

2. In a large mixing bowl, cream the sugar and butter until light and fluffy.

3. Add the eggs to the mixture one at a time, beating well after each addition.

4. Measure out the flour, cocoa, and baking powder in a bowl, then sift them into the large bowl. Fold in gently with a large metal spoon, adding enough milk to make the mixture smooth but not runny.

5. Spoon the mixture into the prepared cake pan and level the surface.

6. Bake for 50–55 minutes until a metal skewer or sharp knife inserted in the cake comes out clean. Check the cake after 30 minutes and if necessary place a sheet of foil on top to prevent it from burning.

7. Leave the cake in its pan on a wire rack to cool completely, then turn out.

8. To make the filling and topping, sift the sugar and cocoa powder into a large bowl and add the butter and 2 tablespoons milk. Mix well with a round-ended knife or electric whisk, adding more milk if necessary to make the butter icing soft and easy to spread. Taste, and adjust the flavor with more sugar or cocoa if necessary.

9. Carefully cut the cake into two layers. Spread a good quantity of the butter icing on the bottom layer, replace the top layer, and cover the whole cake with the remaining icing. Arrange chocolate buttons on the topping, if using.

# My Naughty Little Sister's
# Guide to Cutting Out

**F**OR every angelic child in literature there is a mischievous one. In "My Naughty Little Sister Cuts Out" by Dorothy Edwards, My Naughty Little Sister has a cold brought on by overzealous splashing in puddles and waterlogged rain boots, and she is fidgety, bored, and not tempted by the sewing kit or a picture book. But she does like the sound of her mother's suggestion to create a scrapbook with a "big book with clean pages," old cards and glue, and "nice snippy scissors from Mother's workbox." She cuts out her images "and then she laughed and laughed." In a somewhat demonic way, it turns out.

> *She laughed because she had stuck them all in the book in a funny way. She stuck the lady in first, and then she put the basket of roses on the lady's head, and the cow on top of that, and then she put the house and the squirrel under the lady's feet. My naughty little sister thought that the lady looked very funny with the basket of flowers and the cow on her head.*

Her collage is wonderfully surreal, and similar in concept to the Monty Python visuals and the work of artists such as Salvador Dalí. Her playful, topsy-turvy vision is wonderful, and no doubt many children left to their own devices would soon leave the straight-and-narrow path of everything in its rightful place to experiment with surrealism.

Once rules have been broken, though, the problem is knowing when to stop. After her scrapbooking adventures, My Naughty

Little Sister goes on a scissor-and-glue bender, wrecks the table-top, cards, and newspapers, attempts to snip the cat, and finally cuts up a parcel containing fabric for her bridesmaid's dress. The young reader is alternately horrified and secretly thrilled, and any adult reading is keenly reminded of the need to stay close by when a child is armed with scissors and has a knowing smile on his or her face.

### ❧ PRACTICAL ❧

Children can have plenty of straightforward or surreal fun cutting up old cards before it all goes pear-shaped.

- Collect and/or recycle birthday, Christmas and greeting cards, postcards, magazines, comics, catalogs, old illustrated picture books.

❦ Glue sticks are the least messy option, although many children love using PVA glue in a pot, and brushes or plastic spreaders.

❦ Children's paper scissors are the safest means of cutting (and are useless on fabric).

❦ A scrapbook can be bought or one can be made from sheets of plain or craft paper that can be stapled together between covers made from thicker paper or cardstock.

❦ Cover the work or table surface with newspaper. Spread out the cards and pictures, set out paper/book and glue. Stand back and let the children create. Use the Dorothy Edwards story if you need to make suggestions for pictures.

❦ Stop the activity before sharp scissors and sticking glue are applied to clothing, furniture, curtains, or pets.

# Bad Harry's Birthday Trifle

THERE is an exquisite delight mingled with pain that comes as you read or listen to stories and you *know* without a shadow of a doubt that the main character is going to be naughty. I was the archetypal Sensible Big Sister so I adored *My Naughty Little Sister* by Dorothy Edwards and could never get enough of the heroine's naughtiness, but I also knew that underneath the apparently willfully naughty exterior was a very sweet, natural, curious little girl.

I can still recall the terrified tummy-turning that accompanied my favorite story of all, "My Naughty Little Sister at the Party." She and her partner in crime, Bad Harry, absent themselves from his birthday party at which all the nice little children are playing party games, admire the party tea in the next room, then sneak into the larder where the pièce de résistance, a surprise treat, is hidden.

> *Bad Harry showed my naughty little sister a lovely spongy trifle, covered with creamy stuff and with silver balls and jelly-sweets on the top. And my naughty little sister stared more than ever because she liked spongy trifle better than jellies or blancmanges or biscuits or sandwiches or cakes-with-cherries-on, or even birthday-cake, so she said, "For me."*
>
> *Bad Harry said, "For me too."*

And it is inevitable that they are going to pick off a sweet and a ball, then go deeper and deeper until the whole thing is so "untidy" that they eat almost the entire trifle, and are only prevented from doing so by the arrival of Bad Harry's mother.

My Naughty Little Sister's punishment is a bad night's sleep and a lifelong aversion to spongy trifle, but the reader understands that she has had an experience that many children would repeat, given half the chance and a little more privacy in the larder.

My Naughty Little Sister stories have all the flavor of the 1950s. This was a decade of gaudy, elaborate, and excessively decorated food, and trifles with layers of vivid color and sparkly, sugary, unnatural toppings were made by every chic hostess. I know the trifle has moved on since then but, in the interests of authenticity, and so that you can re-create a taste of the 1950s, here are two recipes for classic, iconic, multicolored trifles. One contains alcohol and one contains Jell-O, but there is nothing to stop you from mixing and matching the layers to suit your preference and guests.

Before making either recipe, first choose your best trifle bowl; the whole point of trifle is that you should be able to see and appreciate the layers through the sides of a glass bowl. It should be large and have a relatively flat base.

## Tipsy Trifle

**MAKES 1 LARGE TRIFLE (SERVES 6–8)**
*6–8 trifle sponges (enough to cover the base of your trifle bowl)*
*Raspberry jam*
*⅓ cup sweet sherry, Madeira, or Marsala*
*2 packages raspberries in fruit juice*
*2½ cups custard, made with custard powder*
*1¼ cups heavy cream*
*Silver balls, hundreds and thousands, glacé cherries, or angelica, to decorate*

1. Slice each trifle sponge open horizontally and spread one side with raspberry jam. Place the tops back on and arrange on the bottom of the bowl. Pour your chosen alcohol evenly over the sponges. Leave to soak for 5 minutes while you deal with the raspberries and make the custard.

2. Drain the liquid from the tinned raspberries and scatter the fruit on top of the sponges.

3. Make the custard according to the instructions on the package. Pour this over the sponges and raspberries and leave until cold. It's best to set the trifle aside at this point for a few hours or overnight so that the flavors develop fully.

4. When you are ready to serve the trifle, whisk the cream until soft peaks form, and spoon it over the custard.

5. You should now have a wonderful, stripy trifle with a snowy white surface, which you can decorate as you please, using silver balls, hundreds and thousands, glacé cherries, or pieces of angelica.

6. Stand back, admire, and serve before anyone starts digging into the bowl uninvited.

## Jell-O Trifle

**MAKES 1 LARGE TRIFLE (SERVES 6–8)**
*6–8 trifle sponges or trifle sponge fingers (enough to cover the base of your trifle bowl)*
*2 packages raspberries in fruit juice*
*1 package raspberry Jell-O*
*2½ cups custard, made with custard powder*
*1½ cups heavy cream*
*Silver balls, hundreds and thousands, glacé cherries, or angelica, to decorate*

1. Cover the base of your trifle bowl with the trifle sponges or ladyfingers.

2. Drain the liquid from the packaged raspberries and scatter the fruit on top of the sponges.

3. Make up the Jell-O with 1⅔ cups water (instead of the usual 2½ cups), and carefully pour this over the sponges and raspberries. Leave to set completely before making the next layer.

4. When the Jell-O has set, make the custard according to the instructions on the package. Allow it to cool a little (otherwise it will melt the Jell-O below) then pour it over the Jell-O and leave until cold.

**5.** When you are ready to serve the trifle, whisk the heavy cream until soft peaks form, and spoon it over the custard.

NOTE: See Steps 5 and 6 of Tipsy Trifle.

# Make a Get-Better Box

Modern children are very lucky to be spared the misery of measles, mumps, and rubella, a truly horrible trio of illnesses. Nevertheless, there are plenty of other illnesses and maladies waiting to strike and turn cheerful, smiley children into miserable, cross, and spotty ones like Dorothy Edwards's My Naughty Little Sister when she has measles.

The patient and kind next-door neighbor, Mrs. Cocoa Jones, comes to look after her and is prompted to remember the get-better box made by her granny for whoever was poorly and needed cheering up; whenever she found something she thought would amuse a "not-well" child she would put it in her box. And so it became a great treat to borrow the box because although you might know some of its contents, there would always be new things, too. Even Mrs. Cocoa Jones finds herself looking forward to seeing it again after many years as she brings it out for the cross, spotty child.

The box looks beautiful and interesting with its covering of various wallpapers from different rooms in different houses, such as Mrs. Cocoa Jones's own childhood bedroom, and it contains all sorts of little treasures, often hidden inside tiny, painted boxes within the box. There's a piece of spangle-covered fabric from a dress worn by a real fairy queen in a pantomime, a little string of beads, a tiny doll, a collection of shells, a little paper fan, "and in another there was a little laughing clown's face cut out of paper that Mrs. Cocoa's granny had stuck there as a surprise," which, sure enough, makes the cross child smile. Then there are picture postcards, some pretty stones (some sparkly, some with holes), a pinecone, pieces of colored glass, a silver pencil with a magic picture in its handle, and a small illustrated book.

Just as Mrs. Cocoa Jones expected, "it amused and amused my sister," who takes everything out and sorts and displays and examines and arranges the contents. And rather touchingly, when she's back on her feet, she chalks red spots on her doll and makes her a get-better box with a boot box "so that she could have measles and the get-better box to play with."

Making a get-better box is a lovely thing to do, both for adults in advance of any illness and for children who can be helped to make their own box of treasures. It's very simple, and requires little more than thoughtfulness, imagination, and the exercising of a magpie instinct.

### CHOOSING AND FILLING A GET-BETTER BOX

- Choose a box that will survive frequent handling.

- Buy a box or decorate a strong shoe or boot box with wallpaper or wrapping paper.

- Collect interesting, unusual items to go inside, and little boxes to go within the big box. Think of a get-better box as a variation on the Christmas stocking theme, but with longer-lasting contents.

### SUGGESTIONS FOR CONTENTS

- Scraps of fabric, nice buttons, beads, old jewelry, false flowers, feathers, stamps, sequins

- Card-making packs from hobby stores and suppliers contain lovely little things—you could include a pack to be used each time the box is needed

- A pack of playing cards

- Unusual little items from foreign countries

- Model cars, planes, toy soldiers, tiny dolls, teddy bears, Russian *matryoshka* dolls, trolls

- Old credit cards, keys, key rings, foreign coins, and banknotes

- Photos, postcards, stickers

- Sea glass, shells, unusual stones, pinecones

- Mini-books, mini-packs of coloring pencils, mini-exercise books, tiny pens

- Scrapbook pictures and paper dolls

- Small, amusing toys, for example, a miniature kaleidoscope, wooden puzzles, and wind-up toys such as walking, chattering false teeth

### MORE IDEAS FOR AMUSING SICK CHILDREN

- Tyke Tyler in *The Turbulent Term of Tyke Tyler* by Gene Kemp enjoys Marvel comics and a bag of sherbet when she is stuck in bed. Secondhand bookstores and charity shops are a great source of old annuals.

- In *The Peppermint Pig* by Nina Bawden, Poll staves off boredom with a scrapbook, a collection of birds' eggs to look at, and a large album of family photographs.

# Jeremy and Jemima's
# More-Jam-Than-Puff Jam Puffs

### ✳

AT first glance it's difficult to believe that the whimsical, lighthearted, and affectionate *Chitty Chitty Bang Bang* was written by the same man who created the often cruel, dark, and sadistic world of James Bond. The two seem poles apart, until you realize that food, fizzy drinks, and cars feature strongly in both, although I suspect James Bond never knew the delights of a clapped-out old car, and he certainly never packed hampers full of jam puffs to enjoy with his Pommery '50.

Ian Fleming relished writing descriptions of food (he once wrote, "My contribution to thriller-writing has been to attempt the total stimulation of the reader all the way through, even to his taste buds") and *Chitty Chitty Bang Bang* is an epicurean delight. Only someone who loved food could pack an imaginary hamper for a day's outing with "hard-boiled eggs, cold sausages, bread-and-butter sandwiches, jam puffs (with, of course, like all good jam puffs, more jam than puff) and bottles and bottles of the best fizzy lemonade and orange squash."

Wouldn't it be marvelous to reenact the story and cross the Channel from Kent to France in a flying car, land on a warm beach to swim and clamber on the rocks, then settle down to enjoy "every single hard-boiled egg, every single cold sausage, and every single strawberry jam puff" before becoming embroiled in a French adventure and being rewarded with the closely guarded recipe for "Monsieur Bon-Bon's Secret Fooj"?

Much as I like the sound of "Fooj" (the French way of saying "fudge," according to Fleming) and am grateful for the recipe provided in the book, I found that what I really wanted to make were the more-jam-than-puff jam puffs that Jeremy and Jemima enjoy as part of their beach picnic. Then I can live in hope that while I am eating them James Bond will emerge from the English Channel wearing nothing more than his swimming trunks.

Jam puffs can be made in two ways: in individual portions or as one large puff which is then sliced. With the aim of having the maximum jam-to-puff ratio, I am giving a recipe for one, large jam-packed puff. But it will also work if you prefer to make a dozen small enclosed puffs, as long as you remember to reduce the cooking time accordingly.

**MAKES 1 LARGE JAM PUFF (SERVES 12)**

*1 (12.5-oz) packet puff pastry (preferably containing
    2 ready-rolled sheets)*
*1 jar jam (whatever flavor you prefer)*
*Milk or water, for sealing*
*1 egg white, lightly beaten*
*Superfine sugar, for sprinkling*
*Whipped cream, to serve (optional)*
*Baking sheet lined with baking parchment*

1. Preheat the oven to 400°F.

2. If you are using ready-rolled pastry, place one piece on the baking sheet. If not, roll out the pastry into a large rectangle about 2 inches thick. Cut into two equal pieces and place one on the baking sheet.

3. Spread the pastry with a thick layer of jam to within ⅓ inch of the edge. Lightly wet the edges with water or milk.

4. Cover with the second sheet of pastry and press the edges together to seal, turning them upward slightly to prevent the jam from escaping during cooking.

5. Bake in the oven for 20 minutes, then remove and brush the surface with the egg white. Sprinkle with the superfine sugar, and return to the oven for an additional 10 minutes until the pastry is golden brown.

6. Transfer the tray to a wire rack and leave the jam puff to cool. When cool, slice the puff into strips, without pressing too hard, and arrange on a plate or pack in a hamper. Jam puffs are also delicious served with whipped cream.

# Make a Toasting Fire

WHETHER you are a child or an adult, there is nothing better on a cold evening than enveloping yourself in a long, woolen plaid dressing gown (or robe) tied with a silky, twisted cord, or a fluffy, brushed cotton version that boasts a good number of interesting buttons, and sitting around the fire toasting yourself. I also think it's a good idea to keep old and outgrown dressing gowns available for visitors so that they can join in the fun of toasting themselves.

Mr. Badger in *The Wind in the Willows* by Kenneth Grahame knows the value of dressing gowns. When Ratty and Mole appear out of the cold and snowy night after their adventure in the Wild Wood, he ushers the freezing and dispirited pair into his marvelously cozy, snug, well-stocked kitchen where he has been enjoying his supper.

> *The kindly Badger thrust them down on a settle to toast themselves at the fire…then he fetched them dressing-gowns and slippers… [and] when at last they were thoroughly toasted, the Badger summoned them to the table, where he had been busy laying a repast.*

A little while later, "they gathered round the glowing embers of the great wood fire, and thought how jolly it was to be sitting up *so* late, and *so* independent, and *so* full."

This little scene sums up everything that is appealing to children about a night in front of a fire (ironically, it's somehow possible to stay up much later when you're dressed for bed). So turn down the heating, put on a dressing gown, and, if it's possible, light a fire and toast both yourself and some food.

## ❧ PRACTICAL ❧

Once children are old enough to be trusted with the operation, it's worth teaching them how to make a fire (or learning with them). There is nothing like the satisfaction of creating a long-lasting, flickering, crackling blaze. Plus, anyone who can light a fire will always be welcome in cold houses.

### FOOD TO TOAST ON FIRES

Toasting food on a fire is one of the most exciting forms of cooking. Here are some suggestions for food to be toasted.

- In *Heidi* by Johanna Spyri, Heidi's grandfather toasts chunks of cheese until they begin to melt and then transfers them to slices of chewy, tasty bread.

- The children in *The Box of Delights* by John Masefield toast bread and dripping and sausages, lying on the hearth in front of a fire as part of their game of Robber Tea.

- Milly-Molly-Mandy, little-friend-Susan, and Billy Blunt enjoy fresh muffins (delivered by the Muffin-man) toasted on forks in the story "Milly-Molly-Mandy Has Friends."

❦ Aunt Harriet makes toast on a brass fork and serves it with dripping, potato cakes, golden syrup, and sticky caraway-seed biscuits in *The Peppermint Pig* by Nina Bawden.

❦ Katie Morag and her cousins toast marshmallows on sticks on an outdoor fire in *Katie Morag and the Big Boy Cousins* by Mairi Hedderwick.

❦ But the ultimate in food to cook over a fire has to be pigs' tails. This is what Laura and Mary do in *Little House in the Big Woods* by Laura Ingalls Wilder. Oh yes, indeed. For more details turn to page 163.

---

### TEN BOOKS TO READ BY THE FIRE IN WINTER

1. *Winter Holiday*, Arthur Ransome (snow and igloos)
2. *The Box of Delights*, John Masefield (Christmas and New Year)
3. *The Rat-a-Tat Mystery*, Enid Blyton (snowy fun and mystery)
4. *Little Women*, Louisa May Alcott (Christmas without presents)
5. *Ballet Shoes*, Noel Streatfeild (Christmas with presents)
6. The Little House books, Laura Ingalls Wilder (winter rituals and fun)
7. *The Peppermint Pig*, Nina Bawden (sliding and skating on ice)
8. *Five Go Adventuring Again*, Enid Blyton (secrets and codes)
9. *A Little Princess*, Frances Hodgson Burnett (cold, hungry heroine)
10. *The Mystery of the Secret Room*, Enid Blyton (Christmas holiday adventure)

# Wind in the Willows River Picnic Cress Sandwidges

ONE hundred years after the publication of Kenneth Grahame's *Wind in the Willows*, the River Thames above Reading in Berkshire where the story takes place remains outstandingly beautiful, and is still one of the finest places for a river picnic from a "fat, wicker luncheon-basket" like the one Rat brings on his outing with Mole.

When Mole asks Rat what's inside, his reply is as crammed as the hamper:

> *"There's cold chicken inside," replied the Rat briefly; "coldtongue-coldhamcoldbeefpickledgherkinssaladfrenchrollscresssandwidges-pottedmeatgingerbeerlemonadesodawater—"*
>
> *"O stop, stop," cried the Mole in ecstasies: "This is too much!"*

*The Wind in the Willows* reminds us that some treats never lose their charm over time; messing around in a boat, a full picnic hamper, a lovely stretch of river, and all the time in the world to enjoy them. Yet we seem to have overlooked one, the "cress sandwidge," and it would be a cruel loss to the joys of river picnics if we were to abandon it altogether. For the cress sandwidge is simplicity itself, and I would guess that everyone, young or old, sailor or landlubber, would enjoy one while sitting in a boat or on a checked wool blanket under a shady tree as time, and the river, go by.

Since we are talking about living life at a more leisurely pace, why not consider taking the time to grow your own cress to put in dainty sandwiches for a picnic? If you want cress for Saturday, sow some seeds on Monday and within five days you'll be able to harvest your own spicy, peppery filling.

FIVE DAYS BEFORE THE PICNIC:
*1 large plate*
*1 packet cress seeds*
*1 roll or pleat of cotton wool*

1. Cover a large plate with a layer of cotton wool. Soak thoroughly with water, then pour off the excess.

2. Scatter the cress seeds over the surface of the cotton wool.

3. Leave in a bright, warm place (a kitchen windowsill is ideal). Do not allow the cotton wool to dry out. The cress is ready to eat when the leaves are fully formed.

ON THE DAY OF THE PICNIC:
*Soft, salted butter*
*Thin slices of white or brown bread*
*Freshly harvested cress*
*Salt (optional)*

1. Spread the butter thinly on the bread.

2. Cut the cress and scatter it thickly on half the slices. Add a sprinkling of salt, if desired.

3. Cover with the remaining slices, remove the crusts, and cut the sandwiches into triangles.

4. Pack in a hamper and take the sandwiches to the river.

# Go Puddle-Jumping in Rain Boots

✳

*If it had been raining Alfie liked to go stamping about in mud and walking through puddles, splish, splash, SPLOSH!*

For more than a quarter century children have been inspired by *Alfie's Feet* to go puddle-jumping and mud-splashing in their boots. This is not to say that Shirley Hughes invented these simple activities; it's just that she was the first to make them look so enticing in her enduring and endearing story. With her inimitable style, she manages to capture one of the timeless joys and pleasures of childhood and turns it into an "I want to do that!" activity.

Such are her powers of suggestion, I'm willing to bet there are also quite a few adults who echo this sentiment when they read *Alfie's Feet*. And why not? Puddle-jumping and mud-splashing keep us young at heart, even if we can't all stay forever young like Alfie.

## ❧ PRACTICAL ❧

🐝 Rain boots are enjoying a phase of renewed popularity which means it's no longer a case of "any color as long as it's black." There are all sorts of colorful and patterned boots to get children and adults puddle-jumping and mud-splashing.

🐝 The beauty of puddle-jumping and mud-splashing is that they can be done anywhere and are great urban and rural activities for little children who need to get out of the house regularly.

🐛 Having said that, there is nothing to stop older children enjoying a spot of puddle-jumping. A friend's family has a New Year's Day tradition: They go on a long walk and the three children (now teenagers) and their friends have a competition to see who can get the wettest while jumping in puddles. Their boots are emptied into measuring jugs when they get home, and a prize is awarded. Warm drinks and Christmas cake follow.

🐛 Another charming perennial rain-boots wearer is Josie Smith in the books by Magdalen Nabb. Highly recommended for young readers and for reading together.

# Enjoy a Dark and Stormy Night

HACKNEYED? Certainly. A cliché? Oh, yes. But there aren't many opening lines that create such a thrill, such a sense of excitement and anticipation, as "It was a dark and stormy night."

There is no better way to enjoy wild weather, tossing trees, lashing rain, howling winds, dark clouds, and moon shadows than wrapped up in a comfy robe while sitting on a bed or by a window (think of *The Sound of Music* and all that lovely night-wear when the children pile into Maria's room during a violent storm). Then, when the storm abates or you have been sufficiently entertained or perhaps terrified by the spectacle, you can go downstairs to a bright and cozy kitchen and have an impromptu midnight supper with the other sleepless people in your house.

This ripping thing to do is inspired by the wonderfully evocative opening scene in *A Wrinkle in Time* by Madeleine L'Engle (first line: "It was a dark and stormy night") when Meg Murry is unable to sleep through the storm in her shivery-cold attic bedroom.

*I'll make myself some cocoa, she decided.—That'll cheer me up.*

As soon as she reaches the kitchen, she finds a lovely contrast to what's going on outside; her brother is calmly drinking milk and eating bread and jam while the dog is lying happily under the table. Their mother joins them and cocoa and sandwiches are made: "liverwurst-and cream-cheese" for Mrs. Murry, tomato for Meg.

*Meg knelt at her mother's feet. The warmth and light of the kitchen had relaxed her so that her attic fears had gone. The cocoa steamed fragrantly in the saucepan; geraniums bloomed on the windowsills and there was a bouquet of tiny yellow chrysanthemums in the center of the table. The curtains, red, with a blue and green geometrical pattern, were drawn, and seemed to reflect their cheerfulness throughout the room.*

Order is apparently restored…

### WHAT YOU NEED

- A dark and stormy night when no one can sleep

- A warm, bright kitchen

- A dog or cat (optional)

- Cheerful flowers in pots or vases

- Dress code: nighties, pajamas, warm socks, slippers, and robes

### WHAT TO DO

- Batten down the hatches, close the windows and curtains, and make the kitchen cozy and warm.

- Prepare cocoa, hot milk, toast and butter, bread and jam, and sandwiches with unusual combinations of fillings (midnight suppers provide the perfect moment to experiment).

- Talk, play cards, listen to descriptions and news of the storm on local radio.

- Read aloud: *A Wrinkle in Time* for older readers, or *It Was a Dark and Stormy Night* by Janet and Allan Ahlberg for younger ones. Both live up to the promise of the first line.

- Or simply take turns telling a story. Begin with the line, "It was a dark and stormy night…"

# Mr. Tumnus's Toasty Tea

Icould, and did, look for hours at Pauline Baynes's original illustrations for *The Lion, the Witch and the Wardrobe*. A poor illustrator can distract from or even distort the text, whereas a successful one enhances our reading; and Pauline Baynes pulls off such an amazing feat of envisaging Narnia that I, and I'm sure many other people, could never now imagine it any other way.

Just look at the details here. The small, crowded but neat room, the softly glowing light emanating from the lamp, the large kettle by the fire. The dresser filled with reassuringly ordinary crockery, teapots, and tureens to suggest someone who enjoys cooking and eating, the full bookshelves of a keen reader. The little eggs in eggcups on the floor, the comfy armchairs, the table set with tea things, and a rather splendid-looking "sugar-topped cake." And, above all, a generously large, blazing fire for making toast.

Because, as Lucy discovers, tea with Mr. Tumnus is all about toast:

> *And really it was a wonderful tea. There was a nice brown egg,*
> *lightly boiled, for each of them, and then sardines on toast, then*
> *buttered toast and then toast with honey.*

As Mr. Tumnus knows, the comfort value of toast should never be overlooked. It is simple and tasty, and custom can never stale its infinite variety. It is also cheap and easy to prepare, which makes it perfect for a cozy tea in a bookish cave. How sharply this snug Three Toast Tea contrasts with Edmund's solitary, selfish gorging on Turkish delight outside in the snow and ice.

Of course, Mr. Tumnus's tea is meant to be a kidnap trap so that he can bring Lucy to the Queen, but the toast thaws his intentions and he enjoys meeting her so much that he confesses and lets her go. She saves herself by being kind and friendly and trusting, passes the toast test, and goes free, whereas Edmund fails the Turkish delight test and is thus trapped by his own greed.

The trick with something as simple as toast is to use really good ingredients: good bread, good butter, good toppings.

All of the following can be made in front of a fire—no need for a kitchen or a grill. So they are just right for students, campers, and centaurs:

*Sardines on toast:* 1 can of good-quality Mediterranean sardines in olive oil, drained, should cover two slices of thick, white, buttered toast.

*Buttered toast:* I am a self-confessed butter snob and I like to be able to taste the butter on my toast, so I use the delicious salted Bridel from France.

*Honey and toast:* I adore looking at all the different types of honey with their gloriously evocative names and have always liked the idea of honey on toast. But—and this is a terrible handicap for someone who enjoys reading about food in children's literature as much as I do—I don't actually like the taste of honey. Having read so much about it, though, I feel I should include it as a classic toast combination.

*Cheese on toast:* My children love uncooked cheese on toast. If you slice a firm cheese such as Red Leicester, Cheddar, old Gouda, or Emmental very thinly and place it on hot, buttered toast, the cheese will melt just enough to be soft and warm.

# Mrs. Beaver's Gloriously Sticky Marmalade Roll

TEA with Mr. and Mrs. Beaver in *The Lion, the Witch and the Wardrobe*—what a warm and cozy contrast to the permanent winter outside in Narnia, and the threat of the evil, icy Queen. We know the Beavers can be trusted as guides to lead the Pevensie children to Aslan because they are kind, welcoming, and hospitable, and they eat good, tasty family food in their snug home, which is full of large hams and strings of onions.

The Beavers cook the children the perfect tea to guard against the cold. There is fresh trout caught just half an hour ago, creamy milk, and as much deep yellow butter as you want with your potatoes. Then there is a sweet treat made by Mrs. Beaver herself, a wholesome dessert guaranteed to please good-natured children, "a great and gloriously sticky marmalade roll, steaming hot."

All the time the children are eating this simple, well-cooked food, Edmund is still thinking about Turkish delight and, as the narrator points out, "there's nothing that spoils the taste of good ordinary food half so much as the memory of bad magic food."

The plain food on the Beavers' tea table is a metaphor for honesty and good intentions, while a taste for sophisticated Turkish delight is rooted in dishonesty and bad intentions. We pity Edmund as he slips away from the warmth of the Beavers' home to seek the Queen and more Turkish delight. Marmalade roll may not be luxurious and expensive, but it is morally far superior.

Marmalade roll is another name for marmalade roly-poly (a traditional British dessert) and uses exactly the same recipe as jam roly-poly but with a marmalade filling. It's an old-fashioned, sweet, and filling dessert, perfect for cold winter teas, and it will fortify you for an adventure in the snow. Traditionally, a roly-poly dessert is steamed for a couple of hours in a cheesecloth or an old shirtsleeve, from which it emerges pale and puffy and damp. But this version is baked; this method takes far less time and has the advantage of producing a roll that is crisp and golden on the outside and jammily, stickily oozy on the inside. And if it's authenticity you're after, then I assure you that steam will escape as soon as the roll is sliced.

SERVES 4–6

*2½ cups self-raising flour*
*Pinch salt*
*¼ pound shredded suet (beef or vegetarian)*
*¼ cup light brown sugar*
*5 tablespoons (approximately) best marmalade*
*Milk, for brushing*
*Demerara sugar, for sprinkling (optional)*
*Hot custard or cold cream, to serve*
*Baking sheet, lightly greased with suet*

1. Preheat the oven to 350°F.

2. Put the flour into a bowl and stir in the salt, suet, and light brown sugar.

3. Gradually add enough water (approximately ⅓ cup) to make a stiff but not sticky dough.

4. Form the dough into a smooth ball then, on a floured surface, roll it out into a long rectangle about ½ inch thick, 6 inches wide, and 1 foot long.

5. Spread a thick layer of marmalade on the surface, leaving a margin of about ½ inch around the edge. Brush a little water around the edges to form a seal.

6. Now roll the dough up (wide edge to wide edge) and pinch the ends together so that the filling doesn't escape during cooking.

7. Place seam-side down on the baking sheet, brush with milk, and sprinkle with demerara sugar if desired.

8. Bake for 30–40 minutes until browned.

9. Slice thickly and serve immediately with hot custard or cold cream.

# Tempting Turkish Delight

✳

IF you have only ever read about it in *The Lion, the Witch and the Wardrobe*, Turkish delight must be one of the most difficult foods to imagine. What you know from the book is that it is sweet and delicious, presented in pretty boxes tied with silk ribbons, and that pieces can be picked up with fingers and eaten straightaway, because Edmund stuffs them into his mouth as fast as he can. But after this there is a huge gap in information; although it's clear that Turkish delight is the stuff of cravings and grown-up special treats, you still don't know how Turkish delight *tastes*.

So how to describe this sweet? Well, it comes in cubes that a person less greedy than Edmund would need two or three bites to finish. These are dusted with a fine coating of confectioner's sugar mixed with cornstarch, so it is inevitable that you will end up with a light covering of sweet powder on your fingers and clothes after indulging. The texture is unique—firm, jellyish, sticky, and lightly chewy. Good-quality Turkish delight melts in your mouth and fills it with an unmistakable flavor of scented rose petals. It's rather like eating a soft, fluffy powder puff with a whiff of perfume bottles and dressing tables.

Traditionally Turkish delight is made with sugar and starch and rosewater, but it also comes in different flavors (lemon, mint, cardamom) and with additions such as nuts (pistachios, hazelnuts). For me, though, nothing beats the original musky pink rose variety, and this is what the recipe below makes. I won't claim that the result has the authenticity of the genuine article, but it does offer a tantalizing taste of the treat that tempts the weak-willed Edmund.

Turkish delight is also one of those sweets that is great fun to make at home, with lots of sugary stickiness and a strange-looking mixture. And there's nothing to stop you from packaging yours in a smart, beribboned box that opens with a pretty white cloud of confectioner's sugar and the promise of being pampered.

**MAKES APPROXIMATELY 3 POUNDS**
*4½ cups sugar*
*Juice of ½ lemon*
*1⅔ cups cornstarch*
*1 teaspoon cream of tartar*
*1½ tablespoons rosewater*
*Pink or red food coloring*
*¾ cup confectioner's sugar*
*Square (8 × 8-inch) baking pan, lightly oiled*

1. Put the sugar in a large, heavy pan and add 1¼ cups water and the lemon juice.

2. Heat gently, stirring constantly, until the sugar dissolves.

3. Bring the syrup to a boil and simmer until the temperature reaches the soft-ball stage (237–244°F). That is, when a small amount of syrup is dropped into a bowl of cold water it forms a soft ball that can be squashed flat.

4. Remove the pan from the heat.

5. Put 1½ cups of the cornstarch and the cream of tartar into a second large, heavy pan. Place on a medium heat and gradually add 3 cups of water, stirring constantly until there are no lumps.

6. Keep stirring as you bring the mix to a boil; it will form a very thick, gluey paste.

7. Now pour in the hot sugar syrup a little at a time, stirring well after each addition to mix thoroughly.

8. Reduce the heat and allow the mixture to cook very gently for 50–60 minutes, until it is pale golden. You will need to stir it frequently to prevent it from sticking to the pan. It will become a very thick, sticky paste.

9. Remove the pan from the heat and add the rosewater and a small amount of food coloring to achieve the shade you desire. Mix thoroughly.

10. Transfer to the prepared pan and spread evenly.

11. Allow to stand overnight at room temperature.

12. The Turkish delight is now ready to be cut up and dusted. Sift the confectioner's sugar and the remaining cornstarch onto a work surface or large chopping board. Turn the Turkish delight out of the pan onto the dusting mix. With a sharp, oiled knife, cut it into ¾-inch cubes. Roll the cubes in the confectioner's sugar and cornstarch mix to coat all sides.

13. Line a box or an airtight container with waxed paper dusted with the confectioner's sugar and cornstarch mix. Fill with layers of Turkish delight separated by sheets of dusted greaseproof paper.

NOTE: If you would rather buy your Turkish delight, I find the best sort comes in wooden boxes and is imported from Turkey. It can be found in specialty food stores and delicatessens all year-round, and in good supermarkets in the run-up to Christmas.

# A Recipe for Disaster

✳

ONE of the most thrilling aspects of children's literature is reading or listening to stories of badly behaved children. I don't mean willfully or maliciously naughty children whose exploits are recounted in Victorian books in order to act as dreadful warnings, but children whose "bad" behavior stems from their willingness to follow their instinct and impulse rather than the codes set down by adults.

These children are the hungry ones. They have an equal hunger for food and for life. Since they often ignore or reject grown-ups' expectations, they are wonderfully uninhibited, and their exploits are immensely exciting to well-behaved, conformist children who would love, just once, to behave the same way.

Pippi Longstocking is a heroine to many and her wild behavior is the stuff of fantasy. How many children, after reading the Pippi books, have wanted to live on their own in a cottage in an orchard in Sweden and eat peppermints whenever they feel like it, bake pancakes (see Pippi's Swedish Pancakes, page 94) and heart-shaped gingersnaps (see Pippi's Heart-Shaped Swedish Gingersnaps, page 96) on a whim, play tag with policemen, and eat buns and drink tea in trees? She is exuberant, irrepressible, and shockingly independent—not only do the adults in the village disapprove of her, so too did many parents when the book was first published in 1945.

So a genteel tea party at the house of her well-behaved friends, Tommy and Annika, is bound to be a test for Pippi. And she rises to the occasion magnificently. From her red chalk makeup and nail varnish, to her startling entrance, to her rush to pile her plate with cakes, add five lumps of sugar to her tea, and then cram the dunked cakes whole into her mouth, she is dangerously, shockingly funny.

But there is more, for Astrid Lindgren realizes that when it comes to food stories, children love a clownish carnival feast, complete with cream pies in the face. In the middle of the party, oblivious to the ladies' mounting disapproval, Pippi suddenly swoops down onto the large, centerpiece cream cake and removes the red sweet from the top with her teeth.

> *But she had bent down a little too quickly and straightened up, her whole face covered with cream.*
>
> *"Ha ha ha," laughed Pippi. "Now we can play blind-man's-buff…I can't see a thing!"*
>
> *Then she stuck out her tongue and licked off all the cream.*
>
> *"Well, that was really quite an accident," she said. "But now the cake is just going to waste, so I might as well eat the whole thing."*
>
> *And she did.*

Just rereading this now made me laugh out loud and reminded me how grateful I am for writers such as Astrid Lindgren who create exuberant, irrepressible, lovable characters whose zest and appetite for life is closely matched by that for large cream cakes. It may not be the best example of how to behave when having afternoon tea at the Ritz, but I would rather hear about Pippi and her enormous, Rabelaisian capacity for enjoyment than any number of stories designed to "improve" my manners. And I know I am not alone.

A centerpiece, Pippi-style cream cake for a genteel party should look like the kind of creamy confection that a clown might throw in the circus (complete with a red strawberry or cherry in the middle, rather like a clown's nose). This recipe fulfills the brief and makes a version of the traditional Swedish three-layer cake, which is filled with strawberries, covered with cream, and enjoyed on a summer's day. Different fruits or a mix of fruits work equally well. Raspberries, peaches, nectarines, and cherries would all be delicious.

**MAKES 1 LARGE CAKE (SERVES 8–10)**

*2 cups superfine sugar*
*1 cup unsalted butter, softened*
*4 eggs*
*1 cup buttermilk*
*1 teaspoon vanilla extract*
*Finely grated zest of 1 lemon (unwaxed)*
*4½ cups self-raising flour*
*¼ teaspoon baking powder*
*¼ teaspoon baking soda*
*3¼ cups cream*
*3⅛ cups strawberries*
*1 red sweet (optional)*
*9.5-inch round cake or spring-form pan, greased with butter and lined with baking parchment*

1. Preheat the oven to 350°F.

2. In a large mixing bowl, cream the sugar and butter together until pale and fluffy.

3. Beat in the eggs one at a time.

4. Add the buttermilk, vanilla extract, and lemon zest and stir to mix. Sift in the flour, baking powder, and baking soda and fold in gently with a large metal spoon until all the ingredients are just combined.

5. Spoon the mix into the pan and bake for 55–60 minutes until the cake is well risen and a metal skewer or sharp knife inserted in it comes out clean.

6. Leave the cake in its pan on a wire rack to cool completely, then turn out.

7. Cut the cake in half horizontally with a sharp knife. Whip the cream and spread about a third on the bottom layer. Reserve one good strawberry and scatter the remaining ones on top of the cream. Gently replace the top layer of sponge.

8. Spread the remaining cream generously over the top and sides of the cake, and place the single strawberry (or a red sweet if you prefer) in the center.

9. Serve immediately.

# Pippi's Tree Party

ACCORDING to Pippi, the heroine of Astrid Lindgren's *Pippi Longstocking*, a tree is a perfect location for an impromptu party. Pippi's garden is full of old scented roses, fruit trees, and "best of all—several oak and elm trees that were perfect for climbing." Having invited the more reticent Tommy and Annika to scramble up the tree, Pippi declares it's the ideal spot to drink coffee and off she runs to her kitchen, returning with coffee and homemade buns.

As it's impossible for Pippi to do anything in a conventional way, she tosses the coffee cups up to the others from her position on the ground like a juggler in a circus, "but sometimes it was the oak that caught them, and two coffee cups broke…Then it was the rolls' turn, and for a long time there was a shower of rolls in the air. At least they didn't break."

Pippi then climbs up with coffeepot and cream and sugar (this is a very refined tree party) and when the threesome have finished eating and drinking, she simply throws the cups down onto the grass "to see if the china they make these days is very sturdy." I may not encourage my own children to do the same, but there is a lot to be said for Pippi's desire for empirical knowledge. She is never happy to simply accept facts from anyone— not even adults—and feels duty-bound to test them in the same way she tests all the accepted rules of childhood. It would be a very hard-hearted reader who didn't take vicarious delight in her youthful anarchy and mayhem.

## ⊷ PRACTICAL ⊶

Who wouldn't want to emulate Pippi and have a tree party? All that is needed is food, drink, a suitable tree, and some basic juggling skills (even Pippi's aren't always that good).

### IDEAS FOR A PIPPI-STYLE TREE PARTY

- If crockery is going to be juggled it's best if it's unbreakable.

- An alternative method of getting food and drink up the tree is to use a bucket-and-string pulley system over a branch.

- Food suggestions: oranges, apples, plums, muffins, bread rolls, plain sponge cakes, and Swedish cinnamon rolls are all eminently juggleable. Parents may balk at the idea of children drinking hot coffee or tea in trees (Annika spills some coffee on herself but decides it doesn't matter), so cold drinks may be more suitable.

# *Pippi's Swedish Pancakes*

ONE of Pippi Longstocking's greatest charms is her "beginner's mind." Zen Buddhist philosophers believe that the way to enjoy life to the fullest is to approach each task as if for the first time, and to bring a freshness and a desire for discovery to each new day. So the untrained, untutored Pippi approaches baking with a completely original and open mind. If a quantity of biscuit dough is too large to fit on a pastry board, why not roll it out on the floor? If an egg needs to be broken, why not fling it up in the air and wait for it to come down into a bowl? If pancake batter needs beating, why not use whichever implement is on hand as long as it does the job, even if it is a bath brush?

Pippi also brings phenomenal energy to her baking and when she makes a pancake for Tommy and Annika it's like a performance out of the circus. An egg lands and breaks on her head, she beats the batter so hard that it spatters on the kitchen walls, she throws the mix on the pan, tosses the cooked pancake up to the ceiling, then hurls it onto a plate. Nevertheless, her ever-admiring audience and recipients eat it and think it is "a very good pancake."

Swedish pancakes are particularly good for beginner bakers to make. The batter can be prepared by adults for children to cook themselves, and older children can undertake the whole process on their own. There is no mystique to pancakes—you just need a good, flat, hot pan and a large spoon to ladle out the mixture. They don't need to be tossed or thrown unless that's your style. And eggs do not need to be caught in bowls in order to be cracked. But it's an impressive trick if you can master it.

MAKES 10–12 PANCAKES

*3 eggs*
*1½ cups all-purpose flour*
*½ teaspoon salt*
*1 tablespoon superfine sugar*
*1½ cups milk*
*Butter, for greasing*
*Sugar, lemon juice, golden syrup or jam, to serve*
*Griddle or heavy, flat frying pan*

1. In a large mixing bowl, whisk the eggs, flour, salt, and sugar until smooth.

2. Gradually add the milk and beat until the batter is smooth after each addition.

3. Heat the griddle or frying pan and grease it lightly with butter.

4. Spoon a ladleful of the batter onto the griddle or frying pan and quickly tip and swirl the pan to make a thin circle.

5. Cook over a medium heat and when the edge of the pancake is dry and the underside golden, turn it over with a spatula or flip it in the air if you feel like doing tricks. Cook the second side briefly. Serve immediately with whatever accompaniment you prefer.

# Pippi's Heart-Shaped Swedish Gingersnaps

**P**IPPI Longstocking might be thin and only nine years old, but she has colossal energy and focus, and she never does things by halves. Take, for example, baking, for Pippi is an enthusiastic and accomplished baker with a brilliantly unorthodox style.

She has no concept of restraint and doesn't bother with the usual kitchen rules, so when she decides to bake gingersnaps, she doesn't make a dozen or two but five hundred, and rolls and cuts out the enormous quantity of heart-shaped cookies on the kitchen floor, "Because you know what?...What good is it to roll the dough on the table when you're going to bake at least five hundred gingersnaps?" How very practical, thinks the child. How very horrifying, thinks the adult.

Pippi's friends and next-door neighbors, Tommy and Annika, visit while she is baking and are spellbound by her almost magical skills:

> *Pippi could certainly work fast! Tommy and Annika sat down on the firewood box to watch. She rolled out the ginger-snap dough, she tossed the biscuits on to the baking trays, and she flung the trays into the oven. They thought it was almost like watching a film.*

And so, in a comically speeded-up Harold Lloyd– or Charlie Chaplin–style scene, she produces five hundred gingersnaps and then off she goes to look for "stuff" outside, and is delighted when she turns up a rusty old cake pan. "What a find! What a real *find*! You can never have too many tins," she shouts.

How could you *not* love a girl like Pippi who bakes like fury, utters lines like this, and gives old cake pans a new home? This is someone who cares deeply about good baking, so I'm quite sure her gingersnaps would be delicious.

Pippi's Swedish gingersnaps are cookies, and quite different from English gingersnaps, or brandy snaps. They are traditionally cut in a heart shape and on this point Pippi, for once, conforms. This recipe makes 40–50 thin cookies, but the quantities can be multiplied by ten should you wish to make five hundred. Swedish gingersnaps are often beautifully decorated with patterns piped on with white icing.

**MAKES 40–50 THIN GINGERSNAPS**
*8 cloves*
*8 cardamom pods*
*½ cinnamon stick or 1 teaspoon ground cinnamon*
*¾ cup sugar*
*2 tablespoons maple syrup*
*2 teaspoons ground ginger*
*6 tablespoons unsalted butter, softened, cut into small pieces*
*3 cups all-purpose flour*
*1 teaspoon baking soda*
*2 baking sheets, lined with baking parchment*

1. Measure out and grind the cloves, cardamom seeds, and the cinnamon stick.

2. Put the sugar, maple syrup, ground ginger, ground cinnamon, and the cloves and cardamom seeds in a medium pan with 4 tablespoons water and heat gently for 2–3 minutes

until the sugar dissolves. Allow to cool for 5 minutes before transferring to a large mixing bowl.

3. With an electric whisk or wooden spoon, beat in the butter, adding the pieces gradually until the mix is smooth.

4. Sift in the flour and baking soda and mix thoroughly to produce a sticky dough.

5. Divide the dough into two or three pieces, wrap in plastic wrap, and chill in the fridge for at least 2 hours or overnight.

6. When you are ready to bake, take the dough out of the fridge and allow it to warm up for a few minutes while you preheat the oven to 400°F.

7. Roll out each piece of the dough with a wooden rolling pin on a floured surface (the floor, if it works for you). I find the best way to do this is to put a layer of plastic wrap over the dough as this stops it sticking to the rolling pin. Roll the dough very thin and cut out cookies with a heart-shaped cutter. Place well apart on a baking sheet.

8. Bake for 8–10 minutes; take care not to let the cookies burn.

9. Transfer the cookies to a wire rack and leave them to cool. Gingersnaps turn crispy as they cool.

# Hurrah for the Circus!

**H**URRAH for the circus! When I first encountered Astrid Lindgren's Pippi Longstocking, she reminded me of a young, madcap circus entertainer. She is manically energetic, exuberant, and eccentric, a sort of all-in-one clown/strong lady/acrobat/juggler/horse rider/tightrope walker. The more I read of her antics, the more I realized she could have just stepped out of the big top and straight into her Swedish village.

If you're still not convinced, take a look at Pippi's circus credentials. She keeps a pet monkey, bakes five hundred gingersnaps at a time, breaks eggs for baking by throwing them up in the air and catching them in a bowl (not always successfully), and is strong enough to lift a horse. Then there's the matter of her appearance, which is uncannily close to a clown's typical getup: red hair, nonmatching socks, patched dress, and shoes twice the length of her feet.

It's inevitable, then, that when Pippi goes to see a real circus she finds herself propelled by some strange force into the ring, to become the star of the entertainment, upstaging Señorita Carmencita, the horse rider; Miss Elvira on tightrope; and Strong Adolf, the strong man. In doing so, she inspires children everywhere to pull on some oversized shoes and run outside and join the circus.

### ✐ PRACTICAL ✁

There is a whole host of simple circus acts that can be done by almost anyone. Most don't require special equipment and are quite safe.

All the following skills can be practiced and perfected in the home circus.

- ⚑ Juggling: Although it's possible to buy juggling balls and beanbags, there are plenty of ordinary domestic or garden objects that can be used when learning (tennis balls, onions, oranges, bread rolls).

- ⚑ Tightrope walking: on the ground on a piece of string. Or tie a length of elastic at waist height between two points (trees, for example) and walk along it, keeping it under your feet. An umbrella can be used to aid balance—and for effect.

- ⚑ Clowning: water fights (with hoses, water guns, or empty washing-up liquid bottles), silly string, helium balloons, balloon tying. It's also good fun to do clown-style makeup with face paints.

- ⚑ Acrobatics: cartwheels, somersaults, handstands, walking on hands, headstands, leapfrog.

- ⚑ Bicycle tricks: wheelies, monocycles.

- ⚑ Strong man: lifting people, objects, pets. Or pretending to.

- ⚑ Dressing the part: tights, tutus, swimming costumes and trunks, fairy wings, wands.

- ⚑ Stilt walking, balancing, human pyramids, trampolining, mime, magic tricks.

# Private Spaces

WHAT is it about big boxes that is irresistible to children? Ever since they were tiny, all three of my children have been drawn more to the packaging than to the contents of boxes. And this makes me wish I'd had a copy of *Betsy-Tacy* by Maud Hart Lovelace in hand when they were growing up, so that we could have talked about what is probably the ultimate in play boxes, Betsy and Tacy's wooden piano box (and I could have been reassured to discover that I wasn't the only mother ever to encourage eccentric box behavior).

> *This was their headquarters, their playhouse, the center of all their games. It stood behind Betsy's house . . . it was tall enough to hold a piano; so of course it was tall enough to hold Betsy and Tacy . . . this was Betsy's and Tacy's private corner. Betsy's mother was a great believer in people having private corners.*

The two little girls make their wooden box cozy and comfortable by decorating the walls with magazine pictures, importing a rug and makeshift furniture, and keeping their treasures ("stones and moss") in a shoe box (another lovely use of a box). It's a special space, rather like a box in the theater, from which Betsy and Tacy can see and be seen, and it can also be a millinery store, a lemonade store, and a sand store. In fact, it can be anything they want it to be and that, I think, is the lure of the big box.

Children don't need much to fire their imaginations; an expensive playhouse is all well and good, but they often prefer something a little less planned. I am sure they sense that a pretty prefab house comes with a catch—the expectation that they should play in it the way that the adults who design and like it think it ought to be used. By comparison, a large, sturdy, empty box offers much more scope for the imagination; once it is emptied of its contents, its purpose is also removed and it can be transformed into something quite different. It may be a house or a store or a hospital or a spacecraft or a den or a bubble or a caravan or a castle—the list of possibilities is endless.

As a box-deprived child, I would have loved a wooden piano box of my own. But a big cardboard box would have come a close second.

## ✄ PRACTICAL ✄

❧ Don't automatically throw away large delivery boxes and don't assume a child is too old to want to play in one. Even teenagers enjoy cutting windows, spray-painting graffiti or decorations on the walls, both inside and out (it's good to encourage their Banksy tendencies), and crawling into a cardboard den with a blanket and a book or a friend.

❧ There are some excellent cardboard structures on the market. They can be used indoors or taken outdoors in fine weather, and can be folded away when not in use. The best range comes from Ecocentric (www.ecocentric.co.uk). We tested their "pod," which is sturdy and large enough to hold two teenagers (at a nice, comfortable squeeze) and therefore fine for smaller children, and is sufficiently underdesigned to allow for full roaming of the imagination. If you want something with a little more purpose, this company also offers a cardboard igloo, a teepee, a den, and a rocket. You can also buy a rocket and playhouse at www.theredballoon.com.

🐝 Alternatively, children can make their own one-off, unique, architect-designed playhouse using a very large cardboard box, scissors, tape, paint, crayons, and a good measure of creative application.

# Create a Doll Family

ADULTS' illustrated magazines have always provided hours of entertainment for children like Betsy and Tacy. The pictures can be ripped out and pinned on walls, cut up and used for collages, or simply altered and doodled on. (Never underestimate the childish joy of drawing mustaches on ladies and extra body parts on men.)

The best magazine-based game I have come across is the one played by Betsy and Tacy (both age five) in Maud Hart Lovelace's *Betsy-Tacy*, who each have a "doll family living in a magazine." They cut ladies and girls from their mothers' magazines and source their men and boys in men's fashion sheets, donated by the local tailor. "They cut the paper dolls from fashion magazines. They could hardly wait for their mothers' magazines to grow old." They give them names and characters, and create fabulously inventive stories and adventures. In a lovely piece of game control, they ensure that five-year-old characters always have all the best times and most beautiful names, clothes, and accessories (and often go to tea with Mrs. Astor and Mrs. Vanderbilt) while the eight-year-olds (both girls have sisters who are eight) live plain, dowdy, unexciting lives.

What's wonderful is the way in which the dolls lie flat and lifeless within the covers until the girls settle down in their favorite, warm, cozy place next to the stove and release them, like genies, and transform them into rounded, vivacious, and animated characters. This idea of a secret, private, flat-packed game, hidden between the pages of a magazine, ready and waiting to be brought to life is utterly delightful. What joy to have a game as flexible, ongoing, and varied as this. How wonderful to be in charge of the fates and fortunes of an illustrated universe. And what an excellent way of recycling paper.

## ❧ PRACTICAL ❧

This game requires very little in the way of equipment. All that is needed is:

- ❦ A cozy, comfortable place to play.

- ❦ One or more players.

- ❦ A stack of color magazines or catalogs or old books with plenty of photos or illustrations of people and accessories that appeal to the players. It's not just for girls, either, as this game can be played with male figures and paper action-men.

- ❦ Paper scissors.

- ❦ Good names; buy or borrow a book of names. (This is a really worthwhile investment—children love using and inventing unusual and exotic names.)

- ❦ Interesting biographies for each character.

- ❦ Plenty of imagination.

# Make a Mixture

IT turns out that my first youthful independent efforts in the kitchen were not as original as I'd thought. I started with the contents of the cupboards in our kitchen, a bowl, and a spoon but no recipe, just a plan to make "mixtures." I would kneel on a stool and shake, mix, sprinkle, stir, sniff, and reel, but I never dared to taste the results, unlike the far more adventurous Betsy-Tacy and Tib, who make "Everything Pudding" in *Betsy-Tacy and Tib*, the second of the series of Betsy-Tacy books by Maud Hart Lovelace.

One snowy evening, when the three girls are left alone in Betsy's warm kitchen, they decide to teach themselves to cook. As they are not allowed to use the oven (Mamma's instructions) they use a frying pan on top of the stove, and start their "everything" mix promisingly with bacon grease, milk, an egg, and flour. Then they branch out with raisins, coffee, tea, tapioca, cornstarch, and soda. It's not long before they gain confidence and add cinnamon, ginger, allspice, cloves, nutmeg (grated), salt, pepper, molasses, bay leaves, vinegar, olive oil, and mustard. By now they are on a roll and in goes oatmeal, cornmeal, farina, coconut, chocolate, cocoa, butter, lard, an onion, syrup, baking soda, baking powder, rice, macaroni, and citron. And then it's time for the final flourish—flavoring—because "flavoring always comes at the end." Not content with just a single flavoring, they gaily throw in *all* the available flavorings: vanilla and lemon and almond and rose.

And then, because the proof of the pudding is in the eating, they taste their mixture. With delightful understatement, they agree, "It's lovely. But we put in just a little too much of something."

## ❧ PRACTICAL ❧

Many children enjoy having the freedom of the kitchen and the opportunity to pretend to be a proper chef or cook or baker.

- ♟ Provide a stool to stand on in front of a work surface or a chair at a table, an apron, a large mixing bowl, and a wooden spoon for each child.

- ♟ Let them choose ingredients from the cupboards and fridge—or select the ones you are happy for them to use, for example, flour, sugar, water, milk, gravy granules, milk powder, baking soda, confectioner's sugar, sauces and ketchups, food flavorings and colors, rice, spices.

- ♟ I find it's best to put out little bowls of ingredients plus weighing scales, sieves, spoons, forks, and spatulas, and let the children decide how to proceed. It is amazing how long these games can last and how revolting the results can be—and how much children enjoy inventing mixtures.

- ♟ Needless to say, this is not the time to leave them unsupervised.

### INVENT A SIGNATURE DISH

Once children have mastered the basics of putting ingredients together, they can move on to more sophisticated experiments that yield edible and tasty results, like the Petie Burkis Special in *The Midnight Fox*, the excellent coming-of-age novel by Betsy Byars.

*Petie was a great eater, and he got an idea for a new food invention. It was called the Petie Burkis Special. He got his mum to make up some dough, and then on top of this dough, Petie cut up dozens of hot sausages and luncheon meats and different kinds of cheese and pickles. Then he rolled it up and baked it, and when it came out of the oven it looked like a great golden football.*

*Petie sliced it right down the middle with a big knife and pushed half over to me. Wonderful-smelling steam poured up into my face. We started eating and our mouths were on fire... Petie was just moaning with happiness and I ate until my stomach hurt.*

Now that I have a hungry boy of my own, I recognize every detail of Petie's culinary experiment. In the boy-world, size and quantity reign supreme, any received wisdom concerning harmony of flavors and textures is ignored, making and cooking are done by eye and not by rules, and consumption of the finished dish is uninhibited and limited only by how much can be taken in.

Although this type of signature dish does seem to have a particularly masculine character, I think every young person, boy or girl, would be happy to invent one of their own. There's something wonderfully liberating about approaching a simple format—here a spherical version of a calzone or folded-over pizza—with a youthful spirit of improvisation and experimentation. Indeed, it wouldn't surprise me to discover that many a successful sandwich entrepreneur has started this way.

### ❧ PRACTICAL ❧

Letting children experiment with food combinations is a fine way to introduce them to basic recipe building and making. Once they have learned how to make something simple, cheap, sustaining, filling, and reasonably balanced, you can be confident they will never let themselves go hungry when you are out or they are away from home. Below are a couple of variations on the Petie Burkis theme, but this sort of experimentation also works very well with breakfast cereals (combinations of cereals, dried fruit, nuts, and seeds) and muffins (use a basic recipe and add fresh or dried fruit, flavorings, chocolate chips).

## HOT BREAD SNACKS

🎋 For a simple version of the Petie Burkis Special, heat a round loaf or large bread bun in a warm (350°F) oven. When warmed through, slice in half horizontally, remove some of the bread, fill the cavity with a mix of ingredients, and replace the top. Return to the oven and heat gently until the filling is warm and melted, like Petie's.

🎋 Petie Burkis-style special: Make a batch of bread dough (recipes on the Internet) or use a commercial pizza or bread mix. After kneading the dough to be ready for the second rising, flatten it gently into a thick circle (like a thick pizza base). When risen, scatter fillings on top as if making a pizza and roll up the dough or bring the edges up to enclose the ingredients. Bake in a hot oven (400°F) for 20–35 minutes depending on size.

# *Play Poohsticks*

I confess that when I first came across the game of Poohsticks, my initial reaction was something along the lines of Peggy Lee's song "Is That All There Is?"

Poohsticks is the game invented by Winnie-the-Pooh in *The House at Pooh Corner* by A. A. Milne. Like Archimedes, he has a eureka! moment when he realizes the pinecone he has dropped by accident into the river has reappeared on the other side of the bridge. He tests his theory that this wonderful occurrence can be repeated, then develops it by racing two pinecones against each other and keeping score. I get the feeling that if he'd stayed there much longer, he would have set up a little betting shop.

It took me a while to appreciate the subtleties of dropping a stick into a river from one side of a bridge, then rushing across the bridge to watch it emerge on the other side, preferably ahead of any other sticks thrown in at the same time by other players. But as I watched my children play the game, I was drawn to the concept.

## ❧ PRACTICAL ❧

Poohsticks is a great excuse to get out into the lovely countryside at any time of year.

- All you need is a stream or small river, a bridge that can support all the players, and some sticks or pinecones (anything that floats and bobs on a current will work).

- Forests or woods like the Hundred Acre Wood (based on Ashdown Forest in Sussex, England) are ideal; look for

details of forests and woodlands on the U.S. National Park Service website, www.nps.gov.

### HOW TO PLAY POOHSTICKS

- Check that the players begin on the side of the bridge where the water flows in and not out (that is, that they are facing upstream).

- Each player must be able to recognize his or her stick.

- All sticks should be dropped—not thrown—into the water at the same time.

- And, as Peggy Lee might have said, that is all there is.

# Anne's Liniment
## Layer Cake

IT is not all sweetness and light in the kitchens of classic children's stories. Sometimes bakers are fallible, and dramatic disasters happen. And when they do, it's very reassuring for young readers whose own cakes may have collapsed to read about spectacular mishaps. So I would recommend that any budding baker read the chapter "A New Departure in Flavorings" in *Anne of Green Gables* by L. M. Montgomery.

Lips are smacked by Anne and the reader alike as she describes to her best friend, Diana, the treats that have been prepared for the visit of the new minister and his wife (Anne's beloved Sunday School teacher):

> *"We're going to have jellied chicken and cold tongue. We're to have two kinds of jelly, red and yellow, and whipped cream and lemon pie, and cherry pie, and three kinds of cookies, and fruit-cake, and Marilla's famous yellow-plum preserves that she keeps especially for ministers, and pound cake and layer cake, and biscuits as aforesaid."*

The pièce de résistance is to be a layer cake made by Anne herself. It "comes out of the oven as light and feathery as golden foam" and Anne fills it with "layers of ruby jelly."

So it is mystifying when the gallantly polite Mrs. Allan's peculiar expression suggests to Marilla that all is not as it should be with the layer cake. Sure enough, she discovers that Anne has flavored the cake not with Best Vanilla but with

Anodyne Liniment which Marilla had poured into an empty vanilla bottle.

Fortunately laughter, rather than serious food poisoning, follows, and it is heartwarming to be reminded that it's the "kindness" and "thoughtfulness" that go into the act of baking a cake that count more than anything. Something worth remembering when your well-intentioned efforts go horribly wrong.

The phrase *layer cake* always makes me think of a cartoonishly huge, striped confection with lavish amounts of icing, which are cut into towering slices at least 6 inches high. It is the epitome of generous North American cooking, the kind of thing that would shock English cake eaters more used to dainty little slices and bite-size fondant fancies.

But a little research reveals that a layer cake is simply another way of describing any cake that has more than one layer and is sandwiched together with some sort of filling—cream, icing, jelly, curd, jam. However, I think any layer cake that emulates Anne's, but without the liniment, should be teeteringly tall and with some form of bright red filling.

My layer cake is a simple Victoria sponge sandwich, but for a four-layer cake I use double the usual quantities and bake the layers in two batches. This recipe makes a two-layer cake, so multiply everything by two if you are making a four-layer cake and give yourself plenty of time to do all the necessary baking and cooling before assembling it. For both versions, you can use more or less cream and strawberries for the filling and topping, according to taste.

**MAKES 1 TWO-LAYER CAKE**

*1⅓ cups superfine sugar*
*1 cup unsalted butter, softened*
*4 large eggs*
*2½ cups self-raising flour*
*A few drops of vanilla extract*

**FOR THE FILLING AND TOPPING:**

*1 medium (9.5-oz) carton heavy cream, whipped (1 large/19-oz carton for a four-layer cake)*
*1 basket strawberries, washed, hulled, and sliced into halves or quarters (2 baskets for a four-layer cake)*
*2 8-inch-round cake pans, greased with butter*

1. Preheat the oven to 350°F.

2. Cream the sugar and butter until pale and fluffy.

3. Beat in the eggs one at a time (add a tablespoonful of the flour with each addition if necessary to stop the mix curdling), together with the vanilla extract.

4. Sift in the flour and fold in with a large metal spoon.

5. Divide the mixture evenly between the two cake pans (use scales if you want to be really precise) and bake for 25 minutes or until the cakes are golden and firm, and a metal skewer or sharp knife inserted into the center of one of them comes out clean.

6. Leave the cakes in their pans on a wire rack to cool, then turn them out.

7. Repeat the whole operation if you are making more than two layers.

8. Once the cakes are cool, you can build up the layers. For a two-layer cake, place one of the sponges on the serving plate and spread half the whipped cream on top. Sprinkle half the strawberries evenly over the cream, then add the second sponge. Put the remaining cream and strawberries on the top of the cake.

9. For a four-layer cake, repeat the process with the remaining two sponges.

# *Make a Liberally Garlanded Hat*

❊

Tᴀᴇʀᴇ's something utterly irresistible about a simple hat, liberally garlanded with fresh flowers. Imagine a profusion of honeysuckle, jasmine, marigolds, forget-me-nots, roses, marguerites, foliage, and blossoms entwined around the brim of a hat whose surface is barely visible. Imagine what it would be like to be the child wearing this extravagant celebration of nature and how much pleasure it would bring to her, the creator and wearer, and to any appreciative onlooker.

We live in a largely hatless age (I don't count baseball caps) and reserve our millinery for special occasions such as weddings and the races, but that doesn't mean we can't enjoy the frippery and frivolity of a floral hat when the fancy takes us, and we have only to turn to L. M. Montgomery's *Anne of Green Gables* for a lovely lesson in hat trimming.

Anne revels in the beauty of nature all year-round, and is particularly fond of flowers. So when she is denied a dress with puffed sleeves, frills, and furbelows to wear to church (even though she has prayed hard for one), she sets off disconsolately, looking far too plain and sensible for her liking:

> *Anne started off irreproachably ... her hat was a little, flat, glossy, new sailor, the extreme plainness of which ... disappointed Anne, who had permitted herself secret visions of ribbon and flowers.*

But Anne, being Anne and highly sensitive to beauty, is soon distracted by a "golden frenzy of wind-stirred buttercups and a glory of wild roses" (and who wouldn't be, when they are described so beautifully?) and "promptly and liberally" garlands her hat with a "heavy wreath of them" and creates an extraordinary pink and yellow "head adornment." We have the wonderful image of Anne making up for the absence of puffed sleeves with a far more arresting accessory.

Anne is too much of an unfettered child of nature for the locals who disapprove of her excess, but I find this makes her headwear all the more appealing. She looks like an embodiment of summer in her May Day–style hat, which is a perfect expression of her inner exuberance and her joy in nature, colors, beauty, and bounty.

### ❧ PRACTICAL ☙

Trimming a hat with fresh flowers is a lovely thing to do on a summer's day. Whether it's just for the fun of it, for a party, a hat parade, or a special occasion, it's quite easy to indulge in a little wild and wonderful millinery. All that's needed is a plain straw boater, some flowers and foliage, and a lack of restraint.

Cheap straw boaters or straw sailor hats are available from Halloween and costume shops and websites.

- On hat-trimming day, you'll need scissors, ribbons, string, paper clips, and thin wire or green florists' wire. Scotch tape also works as a quick fix.

- Gather the flowers and leaves, making sure you leave long stems that can be wound around other stems if necessary. Shrubs and climbing plants with bendy, pliable stems are ideal. Add ribbons, too.

- Try winding a wreath of stems around the brim and use this to anchor your flowers. Use wire and/or paper clips to secure stems and flowers.

❦ Or hold your flowers and leaves in place with a firmly tied or sewn ribbon. You may wish to cover the entire hat, or just the brim.

❦ Wear, model, and take photos.

# Marilla's Zero-Alcohol
# Raspberry Cordial

SOME children's books, like some foods, don't travel well from continent to continent. But L. M. Montgomery's *Anne of Green Gables* has never suffered from a transatlantic gap, and it has captivated, charmed, and amused readers both young and old all over the world. Anne's romantic flights of fancy, unstoppable talk, and daily enjoyment of natural beauty are the stuff of legend. As is the hilarious chapter "Diana Is Invited to Tea, with Tragic Results" which describes the tea party at which Anne gets her new best friend (age eleven) drunk.

She and Diana, both wearing their *second*-best dresses, start out by observing the correct tea-party protocol. They take on the roles of genteel, well-bred lady acquaintances, exchange pleasantries, and are altogether proper and polite. They are to eat some of Marilla's wonderful fruit cake and cherry preserve and, best of all, enjoy something very special which begins with an "r" and a "c" and is bright red. Anne, with her newfound sophistication, claims airily, "I love bright red drinks, don't you? They taste twice as good as any other color."

How easy it is to see in retrospect that red drinks might just spell danger.

So, after they have played in the orchard, Anne plies Diana with three glasses of what she thinks is raspberry cordial, but she herself abstains because she is full after eating apples. A wise move, as it turns out, for Anne has served Marilla's celebrated three-year-old currant wine and poor Diana is soon the worse for wear. But even after she has been taken to task by Diana's mother and banned from seeing her friend, the reader, like Marilla, is overcome by an "unholy tendency to laughter."

All the time I was reading the story of Anne's tea party, I was desperate to taste some proper, old-fashioned raspberry cordial. The very word is something we don't hear too often these days, yet real cordials are easy to make, and taste so much better than any commercial brand. With their jewel colors, lovely syrupy viscosity, and concentrated flavors, they capture the essence of summer fruit and are wonderfully reviving on a hot day. And you can serve a cordial at a tea party to guests of any age, safe in the knowledge that it will not send them home intoxicated.

**MAKES APPROXIMATELY 4 CUPS**
*3 cups fresh raspberries*
*1½ cups superfine sugar*
*Juice of 1 lemon*
*Still or sparkling mineral water and ice, to serve*

1. Check the raspberries to make sure none are moldy. Remove these and any bits of stalk and leaf.

2. Put the raspberries in a large pan. Add the sugar, lemon juice, and 3 cups water.

3. Place on a medium heat and bring to a boil, stirring occasionally so that the sugar does not stick.

4. Simmer gently for 5 minutes.

5. Remove from the heat and leave to cool for a few minutes.

6. Strain the liquid into a bowl. Press down gently on the fruit pulp in the sieve to extract color and flavor.

7. Leave to cool, then pour the cordial into glass bottles or a jug.

8. Store in the fridge and use within a couple of days.

9. Serve with still or sparkling mineral water and ice.

# Learn Poems by Heart

"**D**ON'T you just love poetry that gives you a crinkly feeling up and down your back?" Anne of Green Gables asks the plain-living, unimaginative but very kind Marilla and, in the process, reminds us all of the pure, often physical, pleasure of poetry.

Like many children, Anne adores words. She scoops them up and stores them in her personal cache where they bide their time until they come rushing and gushing out of her, amusing and bemusing those around her. She even adores the sound of words she doesn't understand; as she says of one grandiose poem, "I don't know what 'squadrons' means nor 'Midian,' either, but it sounds *so* tragical."

Anne wallows in the luxuriance of poetry, its glorious vocabulary, patterns, rhythms, and sounds. She chooses works by German and Scottish Romantic poets to learn by heart, and immerses herself in their romance, tragedy, and melodrama, their celebrations of nature and heroic deeds. She commits her favorite poems to memory so that she can always find solace and excitement in their overwrought language and emotions. She shows that children are quite capable of relishing grandiose, flamboyant language and can listen to, read, memorize, and recite poems.

Discovering and declaiming poetry is a highly enjoyable thing to do at home. In fact, home is the ideal place for poetry; children are relaxed and receptive, and their antipoetry barriers are down. So get out the poetry books, laugh at limericks, play with puns, imagine images, and enjoy yourselves. That "crinkly feeling" is one worth experiencing.

Poetry, please:

1. Tyger! tyger! Burning bright
2. The Owl and the Pussy-Cat went to sea
3. *"You are old, Father William," the young man said*
4. She walks in beauty, like the night
5. *In Xanadu did Kubla Khan*
6. I met a traveler from an antique land
7. How do I love thee? Let me count the ways
8. *Season of mists and mellow fruitfulness*
9. If you can keep your head when all about you
10. *Faster than fairies, faster than witches*

First lines from: 1. "The Tyger" by William Blake, 2. "The Owl and the Pussy-Cat" by Edward Lear, 3. "Father William" by Lewis Carroll, 4. "She Walks in Beauty" by Lord Byron, 5. "Kubla Khan" by Samuel Taylor Coleridge, 6. "Ozymandias of Egypt" by Percy Bysshe Shelley, 7. "How Do I Love Thee?" by Elizabeth Barrett Browning, 8. "To Autumn" by John Keats, 9. "If" by Rudyard Kipling, 10. "From a Railway Carriage" by Robert Louis Stevenson.

# *Make a Melon-Seed Necklace*

How many children wind down in summer these days? Truly wind down to the point at which a simple, soothing, repetitive action can while away a whole sunny afternoon or warm evening? I ask this because if they aren't able or allowed to wind down, children miss out on many lovely pleasures associated with having all the time in the world, something that should be embraced and treasured as long as it lasts: the gentle contentment of sitting with friends on walls in the evenings and eating a pomegranate by picking the seeds out with pins, or lazing on the grass in the sunshine and attempting to make the longest-ever daisy chain.

I was reminded of these calm and creative activities when I read E. Nesbit's *Story of the Treasure Seekers*. The Bastables spend a long summer vacation at home, unable to go to the seaside because money is tight, and yet they manage to find all sorts of ways of amusing themselves in the garden. They make tents, play games such as "shipwrecked mariners," and eat coconut candy. They also club together to buy a melon for tea, "quite a big one, and only a little bit squashy at one end. It was very good, and then we washed the seeds and made things with them and with pins and cotton."

And that's all you need when you are young: a slightly squashy melon, pins, needles, cotton, and time.

### HOW TO MAKE A MELON-SEED NECKLACE
- Use the seeds from any sort of melon (cantaloupe, honeydew, Galia, Charentais) except watermelon.

❦ Scoop out the seeds with a spoon.

❦ Wash the seeds in a sieve or colander to remove the pulp.

❦ Pat the seeds dry with a tea towel or paper towel, or leave them to dry in the sun on newspaper or a tea towel.

❦ Thread a sturdy sharp needle with a length of strong thread (upholstery thread—widely available—is best) or use a double thickness of ordinary sewing thread.

❦ String the melon seeds onto the string until it is long enough to pass over your head or fits around your wrist. Add beads for effect if desired.

❦ Knot tightly and cut the ends of the thread.

❦ Or why not develop the food jewelry theme and make an edible necklace?

❦ Make a popcorn necklace using corn popped at home (bought popcorn is too sticky) and a needle fine enough to go through the pieces of corn without breaking them.

❦ Make a cereal necklace with threadable honey loops, Cheerios, pretzels, or any cereal with a hole in the center.

❦ Sweet bracelets are an excellent party activity and treat. Fill bowls with sweets that have holes, and give each child a length of elastic that will fit loosely around their wrist when knotted.

## Make

It's not surprising that so ██
*The Borrowers* and their kingd██
It's a miniature parallel universe, but ██
topsy-turvy kind, and it's all done with a ██
visation; something that will be recognized b██
used spoons to dig soil, string as intravenous dr██
masks, and masking tape for pretend leg waxing.

Mary Norton's details are wonderful. Walls are paper██
old letters, stamps become regal portraits, chests of drawers██
fashioned from matchboxes, and coins are plates. Fuel is kept in
a mustard box and shoveled onto the fire with a mustard spoon,
and the chimney is an inverted brass funnel. Homily knits cotton thread on sewing pins or darning needles, while Pod uses
a hat pin as his climbing stick when he goes out on borrowing
expeditions. The rooms are carpeted with blotting paper (ideal
because it was "warm and cozy and soaked up spills"), and the
Borrowers' luxurious bath is a small tureen which once held
pâté de foie gras. Best of all is Arrietty's bedroom, made out of
two cigar boxes; when she lies in bed she can look up at a wonderfully glamorous ceiling picture of painted ladies in Havana.

This ingenious, small-scale, recycled world is a marvelous
source of inspiration for a child to make one of their own. It
doesn't have to be for dolls or trolls, either. Toy soldiers, small
stuffed toys, model animals, cars, Playmobil characters, and
Lego people all need good-quality housing. The best place to
start is the book itself, then it's just a matter of being imaginative. The real challenge is to do as the Borrowers do: Borrow and
recycle; don't buy.

## a Borrowers' House

...a Bor-
...series
...a safe
...y dwel-
...ds can
...There is
...er about
...ting and
...ght dolls'

...be used;
...e box may
..., by gluing
...g doors. It's
...tacked, and
the contents kept safe, wh... ...n use.

...many children are fascinated by
...m beneath the floorboards.
...of the most imaginative,
...lively spirit of impro-
...y anyone who has
...ps, tinfoil for
...d with
...are

Before children start to decorate and furnish the house, it's a good idea for them to emulate Pod and go on a borrowing expedition. You never know what might turn out to be useful and beautiful, or have an alternative use in a Borrowers-inspired house.

### USEFUL THINGS FOR MAKING A BORROWERS' HOUSE

- Scraps of material and felt for bedding, curtains, covering furniture, rugs, and carpets.

- Small packs of tissues or rolls of cotton wool for beds and settees (cover them with fabric).

- Matchboxes, soap boxes, and small food boxes are ideal for drawers, kitchen units, fridges, baths.

- Pipe cleaners, beads, buttons, toothpicks, cocktail sticks, tinfoil, bits of old jewelry, used cotton spools, tiny containers, safety pins, chess pieces, and pincushions have all sorts of hitherto undiscovered uses—for example, pipe cleaners could be used as table legs or picture frames.

- Buttons, coins, and bottle caps for plates and bowls.

- Magazine pictures and stamps for wallpaper, pictures, and portraits.

- Include bought pieces such as a doll's house, Playmobil, Lego, Barbie, MyScene, Polly Pocket figures, furnishings, and accessories.

- Have glue, stapler and staples, scissors, paper clips, Scotch tape, pencils, and color pens handy.

# The Borrowers' Potted Shrimps

I MAGINE a quirky, improvised doll's house under the floor-boards, the kind a child might put together with all the things that can be found lying around a house (see page 127). It has beds made out of cigar boxes, a wristwatch for a wall clock, postage stamps for portraits, and cotton spools for stools. But best of all, it is inhabited by real, four-inch-high people who come out when it's quiet to "borrow" more things and, most importantly, food.

This is the sublimely imagined and described world of *The Borrowers* in which tiny, doll-like portions of food are served, and in which a single potted shrimp is a wonderful treat. After Arrietty's first borrowing expedition (and meeting with a "Human Bean"), she and Pod come back to their home. As well as roast sliced chestnuts to eat with butter like toast and tea from a hollow oak-apple, there is "a plate of hot dried currants, well plumped before the fire; there were cinnamon crumbs, crispy golden, and lightly dredged with sugar, and in front of each place, oh, delight of delights, a single potted shrimp" served on silver plates—florins for Arrietty and Homily and a half crown for Pod.

If only everyone could appreciate the delight of potted shrimps, singular or plural. They are one of England's greatest traditional teatime treats yet they are in danger of disappearing from its culinary map. The small brown shrimp is relatively expensive, difficult to obtain, and fiddly to peel, but when "potted" it soaks up butter and fragrant spices beautifully.

You can sometimes find small packs of Morecambe Bay online, or you can have a lovely time making your own. You may have to preorder your brown shrimps from a fishmonger, or you can replace them with small pink shrimp. But if you do use the far superior brown shrimp, it's best to adopt a Borrower approach and see each one as a single, delicious treat.

In keeping with this approach, I have borrowed this recipe from Mrs. Beeton. Potted shrimps taste best when their flavor has developed during a day or two in the fridge.

**SERVES 4**
*5½ tablespoons butter, plus melted butter to cover*
*2 blades of mace*
*Pinch of cayenne pepper (optional)*
*Freshly grated nutmeg*
*1 pound peeled brown shrimp*
*Hot toast, butter, and lemon wedges, to serve*
*4 small ramekins*

1. Put the butter, mace, cayenne if using, and a little grated nutmeg into a medium pan and allow the butter to melt gently over a low heat.

2. Pat the shrimp with paper towels to remove excess moisture, then add them to the pan. Stir gently, allow them to heat through, and leave on a low heat for 5 minutes; do not let the liquid boil.

3. Remove the mace blades, divide the shrimp and butter between the four ramekins, and level the tops.

4. Leave in the fridge to cool, then spoon a thin layer of melted butter over the shrimp and allow it to set.

5. Serve the shrimp with hot toast (brown for preference), more butter, and lemon wedges. (I, for one, do not borrow Pod's idea of eating potted shrimp with a slice of boiled chestnut.)

# How to Make a Rainbow

WHEN Eleanor H. Porter's Pollyanna encounters Sir Isaac Newton's prism for the first time, the outcome is wonderful and joyful, but not very scientific. Pollyanna, of course, already sees the world through a lens that breaks the world up into a huge spectrum of color and interest, unlike most people who struggle on most days to find even a rose-tinted lens. And when she visits the bedridden Mr. Pendleton she not only transforms his sickroom into a rainbow-spangled grotto, she also alters his way of seeing.

Pollyanna notices the "flaming band of blue and gold and green edged with red and violet lying across his pillow" created by the beveled edge of a thermometer in the window and exclaims with delight, "Why, Mr. Pendleton, it's a baby rainbow—a real rainbow come to pay you a visit!"

Touched by her enthusiasm for this little rainbow, and knowing that it is made by a prism breaking light up into different colors, Mr. Pendleton asks his housekeeper to bring in a big, brass candlestick with prism pendants on an old-fashioned candelabrum. A string is tied across the window from the sash curtain fixtures, and the twelve pendants are hooked onto it—with spectacular results:

> It had become fairyland...everywhere were bits of dancing red and green, violet and orange, gold and blue. The wall, the floor, and the furniture, even the bed itself, were aflame with shimmering bits of color.

Even Mr. Pendleton is charmed, and it dawns on him that Pollyanna herself is the "very finest prism of them all."

*"Oh but I don't show beautiful red and green and purple when the sun shines through me, Mr. Pendleton!"*

*"Don't you?" smiled the man.*

## WAYS TO MAKE A RAINBOW

There are several ways of making rainbows at home.

- Hang old CDs on a string or washing line outdoors to create natural fairy lights.

- Make a lovely temporary rainbow on a sunny day with a garden hose. Use a fine spray or mist nozzle, make sure the sunlight is shining over your shoulder from behind, and hold the nozzle upward to create a shower. There will be a wonderful rainbow in the droplets, which work as mini-prisms.

- Plenty of rainbow prisms are available on educational websites and in shops, or pretty crystals can be hung in sunny windows.

- If you can find an old pair of binoculars, take them apart and use the prisms.

- Create a water prism by using a clear glass or jar filled with water (a square jar or small fish tank works best). Place the container in a well-lit window in a room that is otherwise fairly dark. By moving the container around you can cause a prismatic effect on the opposite wall of the room.

- Place a bowl of water in a sunlit window and hold a small mirror at an angle in the water. By adjusting the mirror you should be able to create a prism on the wall.

# Pollyanna's Calf's-Foot Jelly

## ✳

EVEN if they refuse to play, I think most people can understand Pollyanna's "glad game" as described and demonstrated in the eponymous novel by Eleanor H. Porter. It's not difficult, it doesn't require any screens, boards, counters, or dice, and it is simply a matter of looking on the bright side, even if we can't all emulate Pollyanna's "overwhelming, unquenchable gladness for everything."

With her positive, unself-conscious outlook, Pollyanna is a wonderful nurse, cheering up the town's previously negative, cantankerous, and grumpy invalids, and she always enters sickrooms bearing bowls of calf's-foot jelly. This intrigued me, because even though I grew up in northwest England, the heartland of the UCP empire (combined shops and restaurants owned by United Cattle Products, with steamed-up windows, huge displays of tripe, and a strange smell of boiled cow), I was never given calf's-foot jelly when I was feeling ill.

Calf's-foot jelly used to be a well-known restorative and an invalid food, commonplace in the days when no part of a cow could be wasted, and even now many cultures still consider this reduction of caring thoughtfulness as the ultimate gesture of kindness. Making it is a labor of love and, as Pollyanna so ably shows, it should be made not out of duty but out of genuine care and interest. In order for it to be fully efficacious it should, of course, be both offered and accepted with a good seasoning of gladness.

I had every intention of testing this recipe, but it would seem that nowadays calves' feet are as rare as hens' teeth. All the butchers I contacted were unable to get hold of any, so I was forced to consider what a modern-day Pollyanna might offer in bowls to console, cheer, and restore—and the answer was chicken soup. Homemade chicken soup has acquired an almost mythical status which can be attributed to its principal ingredient—the kindness and thoughtfulness with which it is made—which makes it a perfect alternative to calf's-foot jelly.

However, I want to share a recipe for the latter for the sake of keeping an old foodstuff alive, and because I feel sure that all the calves' feet in the world do not disappear completely. And I'm also giving a recipe for chicken soup, partly because I have bowed to pressure from people who are disgusted by the idea of the jelly, and partly because the ingredients are readily available.

## Calf's-Foot Jelly

*2 calf's feet*

1. Scald the feet so that the hair can be removed. Slit in two and remove and discard the fat between the claws. Wash well in warm water.

2. Place both feet in a large pan with 12½ cups water and bring slowly to a boil. Remove all scum as it rises.

3. When the liquid is well skimmed, simmer gently for 6–7 hours until the liquid has reduced by half.

4. Strain into a large bowl if you are going to use the jelly for a sweet jelly, or into small bowls if you are serving it to invalids.

5. Put in a cool place to set.

6. Serve with a Pollyanna-ish smile.

# A Modern Pollyanna's Chicken Soup

*1 medium-size free-range chicken*
*2 organic carrots, cut into quarters*
*2 celery sticks, cut in half*
*1 large onion, peeled and cut in half*
*4 bay leaves*
*10 peppercorns*
*2 teaspoons salt*
*Chicken strips and/or noodles or vermicelli and/or chopped*
*    parsley, to serve (optional)*

1. Put all the ingredients in a large stockpot.

2. Add enough water to just cover the chicken.

3. Bring to a boil, then turn down the heat and leave to simmer gently for 2 hours.

4. Taste and adjust the seasoning and strain the liquid.

5. You can serve the soup immediately, either plain or with strips of chicken and/or thin noodles or vermicelli pasta and/or chopped parsley. Or you can leave the soup to cool and reheat it as necessary, with or without additions.

# Enjoy the Heavens Above

S LEEPING outside is one of those amazing adventures that children enjoy in books set in Australia, America, and India. Descriptions of exotic verandas, balconies and roof terraces, balmy nights, starlit skies, and buzzing insects make many young readers yearn to drag their bedding outside and sleep with nothing between them and the heavens.

Despite its far-from-tropical climate, even in Britain the idea is not unthinkable, and there are sometimes nights that are perfect for sleeping out. All that is needed to enjoy the sights, smells, and sounds of a summer's night is the forecast of warmth and dryness, a sleeping bag, and a measure of Pollyanna-ish spontaneity.

When Pollyanna, heroine of the novel of the same name by Eleanor H. Porter, comes to live with her uncompromising Aunt Polly, her bedroom is a bare attic with its windows fastened tight for fear of letting in flies. One night she goes up to bed to find her room as hot as an oven, so she finds a window she can open, happily breathes in the fresh air, notices that the sunroom below has a wide, flat roof, and immediately wishes her bed were out there.

Several bags holding winter clothes are being stored in the attic, and she takes one containing a sealskin coat for a bed and two thin bags for a pillow and a cover. She climbs out of the window, rejoicing in the cool and refreshing air and, with a sigh of content, settles down to sleep. Unfortunately, her nocturnal adventure is interrupted by those indoors who fear a burglar is creeping about on the roof. But Pollyanna's exploitation of a beautiful night is all that is needed to plant in the reader's mind the idea that sleeping rough is not rough at all, but is in fact wonderfully exciting.

## ❧ PRACTICAL ❧

🌱 Choose a warm, dry night but make it easy to retire indoors should the temperature drop or rain fall, or if anyone becomes unsettled by strange noises. Children will probably want an adult to sleep outside with them, which makes this a lovely family activity with the possibility of creating great memories.

🌱 Make up beds on camp beds or inflatable mattresses. Alternatively, bring bed mattresses outside and place on a waterproof groundsheet to prevent moisture from seeping in. Or sleep on raised areas, if available—for example, decking, veranda, balcony, terrace.

🌱 Consider the alternative of using a bivouac sack (bivy bag) and sleeping mat to turn the night into a real survival adventure by sleeping farther away than the backyard. While I realize this may not appeal to all adults and children, for some a hike or walk over beautiful countryside and a campfire or picnic supper followed by sleeping under the stars is the best way to enjoy the great outdoors.

🌱 Sleeping outside for a night or two is permitted in many parts of the country, but check with the relevant authority/website before you set off.

# *Heidi's Grandfather's Simple Swiss Cheese and Bread Supper*

I F there was one book that made me want to renounce all my worldly goods (trolls, dolls, Fuzzy Felt, Monopoly board) and move to the mountains to live a plain and good life, that book was *Heidi* by Johanna Spyri. When I first read it, I was entranced by the possibility of supreme simplicity in the Swiss Alps; there is something powerfully seductive about the idea of living in a hut, sleeping on a bed of hay in a loft, spending your days in the company of Peter and the goats, and picking pretty primulas to put in your apron pocket.

Not to mention the Swiss bread and cheese. I would even have traded my weekly packet of Opal Fruits, bought with my "spends," for a taste of the plain but intensely evocative meals that Heidi enjoys with her grandfather. Although she is thrilled with the luxury of white bread rolls in Frankfurt, it is the dark, long-lasting bread, enjoyed with cheese and fresh, steaming goats' milk, that comes to symbolize all she missed when she is taken away from her beloved mountains.

Heidi and her initially none-too-welcoming grandfather bond over their first supper together; Heidi watches him prepare the toasted cheese to go with the round bread: "As the pot began to sing, he put a large piece of cheese on a toasting fork and moved it to and fro in front of the fire until it became golden yellow all over."

Their suspicions about each other begin to fade as they share this significant meal, and the unwanted five-year-old Heidi begins to charm her grumpy grandfather with her sweet and sincere nature. It's as if his resistance melts with the cheese...

*Sourdough bread or rye bread*
*Fresh milk (goats' milk optional)*
*Gruyère cheese, cut into 1-inch cubes*
*Long-handled fork or toasting fork*

1. Imagine you are in a wooden hut on the side of a snowy mountain. You can see the stars shining brightly in the clear night sky. Worries, work, mortgages, and bills do not exist for the moment.

2. Stoke the fire until red and glowing.

3. Slice the bread thickly.

4. Pour the fresh milk into mugs.

5. Place a piece of cheese on the fork and swivel and turn it until it bubbles all over and turns a darker, golden color.

6. Transfer quickly to a slice of bread.

7. Eat while hot. Repeat as necessary.

# Treasure Hunting

THERE can be few more potent themes in children's books than that of hidden treasure. Looking for and unearthing a heavy chest of glittering coins or a huge cache of sparkling jewels, solid gold ingots, priceless paintings, or stolen silverware is at the heart of countless thrilling tales. Throw in maps and clues, pirates and smugglers, red herrings and wild-goose chases, plus the possibility of being rich beyond one's wildest dreams, and it's no wonder it's a formula that has been worked and reworked over and over again.

The idea of finding or stumbling upon treasure is one that permeates children's ordinary lives, too. They believe with touching faith that unheard-of wealth *can* be found by chance or by following clues, that rags-to-riches stories *do* come true, and that there's a high possibility of finding treasure in any back garden or on any beach. And this is why organized treasure hunts are perennially popular: They guarantee that treasure will be found. Plus, children are always happy to practice looking for it, because they know that the world is full of undiscovered treasure.

## ☙ PRACTICAL ❧

There are several types of treasure hunts. The first is the Robert Louis Stevenson's *Treasure Island* version, which follows cryptic clues (and sometimes a map) until the treasure is located. The second is simply a matter of finding treasure hidden in various spots by searching a given area. And the third is looking for a set list of items or "treasure." In all cases, winners and finders are rewarded with a piece of treasure: money, sweets, chocolate, or whatever you care to call treasure.

❦ *Treasure Island* hunt: suitable for older children or children working in pairs. To be a success, this type of treasure hunt requires a fair degree of planning and organization. Draw up a map to show the location of the clues, or set and hide clues that lead on from each other. Devise clever/cryptic clues that test the hunters' knowledge of the location or their general knowledge or powers of observation.

❦ Hidden treasure: This is easy and great fun. Hide treasure in various spots around the house or garden or the hunt location (if necessary, make a note of where you have put it—it's very easy to forget). When our children were young, we used to do three variations of this type of hunt: one in wherever we were staying on vacation, making the most of the unusual location, one for Easter, and one for Halloween. The last was the highlight of Phoebe's birthday party: We hid treasure around the garden, waited till it was dark, gave every child a flashlight (very cheap from hardware stores and they doubled as the "going home" present), and let them loose outside.

❦ Treasure gathering: This is a great way to make the most of being outside, in the park, going for a walk, or spending time at the beach. Make a list of "treasure" to be collected by the hunters, who can seek individually or in teams, and either hand out the lists or call out what has to be found. The first team/person to collect everything is the winner. On a walk, treasure could be: certain types of leaves (by tree type, color), horse chestnuts, acorns, pinecones, insects, feathers, pickable flowers such as daisies or buttercups in the wild, pieces of moss, something beginning with a certain letter. In your garden, it could be balls, certain garden flowers (by name, color), fruits, leaves (by type, color, or smell, for example, lavender or mint), ten pieces of gravel, a lost shoe, fallen branches, seeds, pets. On a beach, set children looking for: certain shapes and colors of pebbles, sea glass, shells, dead fish, pieces of orange rope, seaweed, lollipop sticks, something that sinks/floats.

🍎 Children also enjoy digging for treasure, like the Bastables in E. Nesbit's *Story of the Treasure Seekers*, who dig a huge hole in their back garden (many parents may prefer major hole digging to be done at the beach).

🍎 They also like "Turnupstuffing," as Astrid Lindgren's Pippi Longstocking calls it, which is general foraging and poking about looking for what some people would call rubbish and others might call treasure. Turnupstuffing is a great way of adding interest to a walk. When it's done on a beach, it becomes beachcombing.

# Mary Poppins's Strike-Me-Pink
# Raspberry Jam Cakes

*WHEN* it comes to the printed page versus the animated screen, I am of the persuasion that an original book is always better than a derivative film. I'm not saying there aren't some wonderful films based on children's classics; it's just that nothing can ever, ever beat the pictures and images and tastes you create in your own imagination when you're engrossed in a wonderful book.

Mary Poppins is a fine example of the slippage between book and film. Some adults are shocked when they encounter the vain, acerbic, and often bad-tempered literary Mary Poppins for the first time, for she is far removed from the magical, appealing, sweet-voiced Julie Andrews. And she has a much larger appetite.

In *Mary Poppins*, she and Bert jump into an idyllic chalk pavement scene he has created, and are whisked away to "a little open space filled with sunlight."

*And there on a green table was Afternoon Tea!*
*A pile of raspberry jam cakes as high as Mary Poppins' waist stood in the center, and beside it tea was boiling in a big brass urn. Best of all, there were two plates of whelks and two pins to pick them out with.*
*"Strike me pink!" said Mary Poppins. That was what she said when she was pleased.*

In a delightfully extravagant and markedly un-Poppins-ish manner (to those who still think of her as the film version), she and Bert proceed to work their way through the whelks, drink three cups of tea, and eat the entire heap of cakes together.

Raspberry jam cakes sound delicious, don't they? And yet, even though I had never in reality eaten any like the ones Mary Poppins enjoys, I *had* in my imagination. They came on a doily on a proper cake plate, and were dusted with confectioner's sugar. They were small enough to be eaten in two or three dainty bites, and in large quantities. They were pale yellow, sweet, softly spongy with a contrasting fresh, acidic burst of raspberry in the center. They were not too sticky (Mary Poppins does not get sticky after eating sweet cakes) and they were not too filling. And they always elicited cries of "Strike me pink!"

These raspberry cakes sounded so good to me that I had to make some. I searched and searched for a recipe, and eventually I found one in an old cooking magazine that belonged to my mother-in-law, and I have brought this up to date.

**MAKES 12 CAKES**

*2½ cups self-raising flour*
*1 teaspoon baking powder*
*½ cup superfine sugar, plus extra for sprinkling*
*5½ tablespoons butter*
*1 large egg, beaten*
*2–3 tablespoons milk, plus extra for brushing*
*6 teaspoons raspberry jam*
*Tea, to serve*
*Baking sheet, greased with butter or lined with baking
    parchment*

1. Preheat the oven to 350°F.

2. Sift the flour and baking powder into a large bowl. Stir in
   the sugar. Rub in the butter until the mixture resembles
   fine bread crumbs.

3. Add the beaten egg and enough milk to make a soft
   dough. On a lightly floured work surface, shape into a flat-
   tish rectangle and divide into roughly equal pieces with a
   knife. Roll each piece into a ball.

4. Flatten each ball slightly, then make a little depression in
   the center and bring the edges up, as if you were making a
   very basic clay pot. Place ½ teaspoon of the raspberry jam
   in the middle of each cake.

5. With your fingers, gently bring the edges together to close
   the dough over the jam. Then turn the cakes over and place
   them well apart on the baking sheet.

6. Brush the tops with milk and sprinkle each cake with a
   little superfine sugar.

7. Bake in the oven for 15–20 minutes until the cakes are pale gold, but not brown. Do not overcook them, as you want to keep them relatively moist. If you cook them too long they become biscuity.

8. Transfer the tray to a wire rack and leave the cakes to cool.

9. Pile them on a plate and serve with tea.

# Chalking It Up

✳

SOMETIMES it's the simple, tried-and-tested things that are the best. Take chalk, for example. Chalk may seem like something out of the dark ages these days, but I urge you to reconsider its merits. Just think of all that can be done with a cheap box of chalk. People can be taught how to read, write, and do sums on blackboards. Children can enjoy endless games of hopscotch on outdoor surfaces. They can create spectacular wall graffiti. They can attempt to chalk artistic portraits to earn a penny or two. And they can emulate Bert the Match Man in P. L. Travers's *Mary Poppins* and make wonderfully realistic pavement pictures, pictures that are worthy of being hung in the Royal Academy, according to Mary Poppins.

A piece of pavement or path or playground or wall, and a few pieces of chalk, are all children need to create a window on a different world. Drawing and coloring and playing with chalk is oh so simple, but completely absorbing, creative, and as interactive as you like. In fact, I'd bet that quite a few adults would still be more than happy to pick up a few pieces of chalk themselves, get their hands dusty, and hop, skip, and jump back into old times.

### ❦ PRACTICAL ❧

❦ Chalk is amazingly versatile and has all sorts of uses, especially when something washable, nonpermanent, and nontoxic is needed.

❦ Chalk is essential for hopscotch.

❦ And for making pavement pictures.

- And for chalking lines for tightropes, goal areas, tennis courts, volleyball courts, territories, and magic circles.

- Chalk is worth taking or buying on vacation because it can be put to so many uses. For example, pebbles can be dotted with chalk and used to play dominoes on the beach.

- And dolls can be spotted with chalk to make them ill with measles or chickenpox.

- When the chalk pictures or graffiti or grids are no longer needed, they can be washed off with warm water and a scrubbing brush. The cleaning-up process can be a great excuse for a water fight.

- Finally, children still love blackboards even though they are almost obsolete in schools. Together with a box of chalk, a blackboard can enable all sorts of entertaining role-playing games.

# Mrs. Persimmon's Crumpets

CRUMPETS are the backbone of any good afternoon tea party—even when the party is an extraordinary one, eaten at a table floating in the air while you take care not to bump your head on the ceiling.

Mr. Wigg's birthday tea party in *Mary Poppins* appears at first to be very normal; it includes crumpets and there is nothing more solidly sensible and earthbound than a good, old-fashioned English crumpet. When Jane and Michael enter Mr. Wigg's large, cheerful room, they survey the scene:

> *At one end of it a fire was burning brightly and in the center stood an enormous table laid for tea—four cups and saucers, piles of bread and butter, crumpets, coconut cakes and a large plum cake with pink icing.*

But it isn't long before this apparently ordinary tea party turns topsy-turvy due to an uncontrollable excess of laughing gas. The participants float to the ceiling, eat their tea in the "wrong" order—cake first, not sandwiches—and the adults behave like children. It is the epitome of a joyful tea party with good company, good food, lots of laughter, and a complete and enjoyable loss of adult dignity.

Crumpets are the stuff of cold days, warm fires, and toasting forks, and are soft, filling, and comforting. So it is ironic that in this story they are made by the thin, disapproving, and very dignified Mrs. Persimmon, and the episode simply demonstrates how much she is missing out on in life when she refuses to rise to the occasion and join in with crumpets and laughter.

It's best to allow 2½–3 hours from starting the recipe to eating the hot crumpets.

MAKES APPROXIMATELY 18 CRUMPETS
*1 teaspoon active dry yeast or 2½ teaspoons fresh yeast*
*1 teaspoon runny honey*
*2¾ cups lukewarm milk and water (half and half)*
*2⅓ cups all-purpose flour*
*2⅓ cups bread flour*
*2 teaspoons salt*
*¾ teaspoon cream of tartar*
*½ teaspoon baking soda*
*Oil, for greasing*
*Butter, jam, golden syrup, maple syrup, or cheese, to serve*
*4-inch crumpet rings, well oiled; griddle or heavy-based frying pan, lightly oiled*

**1.** Put the yeast into a medium bowl and add the honey and 2 cups of the lukewarm milk and water. Mix well until the yeast has dissolved into the liquid and the honey is mixed in. You should start to see little frothy bubbles appear on the surface immediately; this is a good sign that your yeast is alive and well. If this doesn't happen, you will need to start again with a new batch of yeast.

2. In a large mixing bowl, mix the flours, salt, and cream of tartar. Pour the yeasty liquid into the flour and mix well to make a thick, smooth batter. Cover with plastic wrap or a damp tea towel and leave to stand in a warm place until the batter rises and its surface is covered with bubbles. This will take 1½–2 hours.

3. Dissolve the baking soda in the remaining lukewarm milk and water and stir thoroughly into the batter. Leave in a warm place for an additional 30–45 minutes by which time the surface should once again be covered with little bubbles.

4. You are now ready to cook the crumpets. First, it's best to make sure your batter isn't too thick or too thin by cooking a test crumpet. If your batter is too thin and runs out from under the ring, add a little more flour to the mix. If small holes do not form on the surface, your batter is too thick, in which case you need to add a little more water to loosen the mix.

5. Heat the griddle or frying pan over a moderate heat, then place the rings on it. Spoon or ladle batter into each ring—it's up to you how thick you want your crumpets to be, but I find that slightly thinner ones, about ¼–½ inch thick, are best. Turn the heat up for a couple of minutes to ensure plenty of bubbles form, then reduce the heat and cook gently until the surface of the crumpet is dry and set, and covered with holes—this should take 5–8 minutes.

6. Now ease the rings off, flip the crumpets over, and cook for a further 3 minutes; the holey side is meant to be paler and softer than the underside. The crumpets can be eaten immediately, or wrapped in a cloth or kept in a covered dish while you make more batches.

7. Crumpets are undeniably best when fresh and, to my mind, when served with medically dangerous amounts of butter. Homemade crumpets are best eaten fresh as they begin to get rubbery with age.

# Mrs. Banks's Bribery and Corruption Cocoanut Cakes

In the opening chapter of *Mary Poppins Comes Back*, Mrs. Banks is at her wits' end. Ever since Mary Poppins left without a "Word of Warning," everything is wrong. The water's too hot, the coffee's too cold, nursery nurses have come and gone in quick succession, and now it looks like even Mr. Banks has left for good. Ellen, the maid, has taken to her bed with a "broken leg" and the children's behavior in the nursery has descended into anarchy. So Mrs. Banks does what any sensible mother would do and sends all four children out to the park until teatime with the bribe of something nice to eat: "If you will go quietly and be good children there will be cocoanut cakes for tea."

And, like good children who know when they have the upper hand, they go off to the park to fly Michael's kite. Except the kite changes and in its place dances a familiar figure; it is, of course, Mary Poppins who has come back.

In the blink of an eye because "as usual, everything that Mary Poppins did had the speed of electricity," order, peace, and harmony are restored in the Banks' household. But the downside is that when Jane and Michael come to eat their coconut cakes they do so in super-quick time, which is no doubt a Poppins-ish form of retribution for letting themselves be corrupted by a sweet treat.

It's a shame that all things coconutty are seen as slightly passé these days, as coconut gives a lovely flavor and dampness to sponge cake. Plus, I think all children should experience the pleasure of idly picking little flecks of coconut flesh out of their teeth after eating a cake or two.

If possible, used shredded coconut rather than desiccated coconut as it is sweeter and softer.

**MAKES 12 COCONUT CAKES**
½ cup (1 stick) unsalted butter, softened
⅔ cup superfine sugar
2 eggs
1 cup self-raising flour
½ teaspoon baking powder
⅔ cup shredded or desiccated coconut
2 tablespoons milk
Silver balls or coconut-flavored jelly beans, to decorate
    (optional)

**FOR THE TOPPING:**
2 tablespoons unsalted butter, softened
1⅓ cups confectioner's sugar
⅓ cup shredded or desiccated coconut
2–3 teaspoons milk
1 12-muffin pan and 12 paper liners

1. Preheat the oven to 350°F and place the paper liners in the muffin pan.

2. In a large mixing bowl, cream the butter and sugar until pale and fluffy.

3. Beat in the eggs.

4. Sift the flour and baking powder over the mix, add the coconut and milk, and fold in gently with a large metal spoon.

5. Divide the mix equally between the paper liners and bake for 15–20 minutes until the cakes are golden and their centers feel springy.

6. Leave the cakes in the muffin pan on a wire rack until completely cold.

7. To make the topping, cream together the butter, confectioner's sugar, and coconut, adding enough milk to make the mixture soft. Spread on top of the cakes.

8. A few silver balls or coconut-flavored jelly beans on top of each cake may act as added incentives to good behavior.

# *Watch a Spider Spin a Web*

**M**ANY children in books have action-packed, adventure-filled summers in which they dash about all over the place barely pausing for breath, which is, of course, why so many children whose lives are far less exciting adore reading about them. But, for children whose summers pass at a more leisurely pace, it's reassuring to know that slow and gentle is also good, because childhood is one of the few times in life when you can sit and contemplate your navel, or enjoy some lovely, slow activity such as web weaving all day long should you wish.

E. B. White's *Charlotte's Web* teaches patience and the value of taking your time, and Fern is an excellent pupil. In the summer of the story she visits Wilbur the pig, Charlotte the spider, and the other animals in the barn almost every day: "Charlotte liked to do her weaving during the late afternoon, and Fern liked to sit nearby and watch." By sitting still, and watching and observing nature, she becomes a part of it and the barn becomes a quiet, peaceful, and trusting place. But Fern's mother is so worried about her going there instead of playing with other children that she confides in the doctor who replies, "How enchanting! It must be real nice and quiet down there."

His is the voice of reason; his advice is to let Fern be and, sure enough, by the time the next summer comes around, Fern thinks her behavior was all very childish and bears out the doctor's observation that "it's amazing how children change from year to year."

Nevertheless, the book remains a delightful lesson in not rushing children into growing up but letting them do it in their own time.

# Wake-Up-and-Smell-the-Bacon Breakfast with Hash Browns

I would much prefer to be told to "wake up and smell the coffee" than "pay attention to what's going on around you and do something about it." The phrase is gentle and appealing, rather like the smell of coffee itself. Although it was popularized by the American advice columnist Ann Landers, in the title of her book published in 1996, it would seem that the metaphor was known to E. B. White and Fern, the heroine of *Charlotte's Web*, long before then.

I have noticed that very few children's writers deal with the sense of smell, but *Charlotte's Web* stands out in a generally aroma-free genre. Warm, earthy, farmyardy smells pervade the book, and they draw the reader into the farm, the house, and the story, nose in air and sniffing.

The first chapter begins with some lovely aromas. It is a clever touch to have the farmhouse kitchen smelling mouthwateringly of bacon just as the young Fern Arable decides to prevent her father from killing a small, weak newborn piglet. Having saved Wilbur's bacon, so to speak, she goes back into the house and "the kitchen table was set for breakfast, and the room smelt of coffee, bacon, damp plaster, and wood-smoke from the stove."

And there you are, sitting in a farmhouse in Maine, surrounded by enticing, natural smells, all ready to hear what happens to Wilbur. Will he, or won't he, become just another breakfast dish?

Although I am sure that this story may have put some readers off bacon forever, it does the opposite to me, and makes me wish I could wake up to the delicious smell of coffee and bacon every day.

It's worth buying best-quality, traditionally cured bacon that has come from pigs that have been well looked after; once you have tasted it, there is no going back to the plastic-wrapped, anonymous supermarket version. The taste, the texture, and, above all, the smell cannot be beat.

Such excellent bacon turns an ordinary breakfast into a treat. So why not go the whole hog, if you'll pardon the expression, and treat yourself to a wonderful breakfast, the kind that would be enjoyed in a farmhouse in Maine in the 1950s? Add scrambled eggs, freshly made coffee, and the extra flourish of homemade hash browns, cooked in the bacon fat as in the recipe below.

Then simply wake up and smell it all.

SERVES 4–6
*4 medium potatoes*
*2–3 tablespoons leftover bacon fat*
*Plenty of salt and pepper*

1. Peel and grate the potatoes.

2. Heat the bacon fat in a large, heavy frying pan.

3. When the fat is hot, tip in the potatoes and spread them to form a layer on the base of the pan, pressing down with a spatula to flatten. Season well with salt and pepper.

4. Cook on a medium heat for 6–8 minutes.

5. Cut the circle in half with the spatula, and turn each half over and season again.

6. Cook for an additional 6–8 minutes or until the potatoes are crisp and brown on the bottom.

# Make a Rope Swing

*Mr. Zuckerman had the best swing in the county. It was a single long piece of heavy rope tied to a beam...at the bottom of the rope was a fat knot to sit on. It was arranged so that you could swing without being pushed. You climbed a ladder to the hayloft. Then, holding the rope, you stood at the edge...then you straddled the knot, so that it acted as a seat...then you got up all your nerve... and jumped.*

Few families have a huge barn with what looks like a twenty-foot drop in which to swing, but there can't be many children who don't love the sensation of sailing and twisting and turning and zooming through the air. It's one of those things that is guaranteed to make the onlooker feel more terrified than the person doing it; the child gets the adrenalin rush while any adults watching get the burden of acute anxiety.

If you're still nervous about the idea of children and swings, consider what E. B. White says in *Charlotte's Web*. He makes the excellent and very astute observation that the vast majority of children have absolutely no intention of not holding on tightly, ✓ and that children do not get on a swing with the express aim of falling off and hurting themselves (in fact, the only time they let go deliberately is to land in water or bales of hay).

*Mothers from miles around worried about Zuckerman's swing. They feared some child would fall off. But no child ever did. Children almost always hold on to things tighter than their parents think they will.*

E. B. White recognizes that the stomach-churning joys of swings create some of the best moments of childhood, and that you don't need much in order to get the best out of the concept. Some space, a rope, a high beam, or a strong branch are enough, and if these happen to be over something soft to land on or a stream or pool to fall in, then it's all the better for everyone, swinger and spectators alike.

# This Little Piggy... Roast Pigs' Tails

❊

I don't know whether to laugh or recoil at the idea of roasting a pig's tail over a fire, but there's no doubt it intrigues me. I imagine many a child would be delighted to indulge in a little gory play before plunging a stick or skewer into the thick end of a pig's tail, holding it over a fire, and watching as the fat drips, bubbles, and crackles over the flames and the skin turns dark and crispy, then eating it.

You might be surprised to find that this treat comes from the apparently sweet and charming *Little House in the Big Woods* by Laura Ingalls Wilder. Except that beneath the book's sweetness and charm there is a story of difficult, often harsh, pioneering self-sufficiency, and many a battle with elements and enemies. And in this situation, should you be lucky enough to own or receive a pig, you make sure you eat all of it.

When Pa decides to kill the pig he's been fattening for winter, it's a huge family event. Pa saves the bladder and the tail for Laura and Mary; he makes a balloon out of the bladder (another excellent thing to do at butchering time), "but even better fun was the pig's tail." Pa skins it, pushes a sharp stick into the thick end, and the girls take turns in holding it over coals.

*It sizzled and fried. And drops of fat dripped off and it blazed on the coals. Ma sprinkled it with salt. Their hands and faces got very hot... At last it was done. It was nicely browned all over, and how good it smelled! They carried it into the yard to cool it, and even before it was cool enough they began tasting it and burned their tongues. They ate every little bit of meat off the bones... and that*

163

*was the end of the pig's tail. There would not be another one till*
*next year.*

Marvelous.

### ⤬ PRACTICAL ⤬

If you don't feel squeamish about handling pigs' tails (or bladders), roasting them in the simple and easy Little House–style over coals or a fire would be a brilliantly entertaining and memorable thing to do.

# Ma's Pancake Men

I am a great fan of American-style pancakes. I was converted years ago by a huge stack of the lightest, fluffiest pancakes at Lou Mitchell's Café in Chicago. Ever since then, I have forsworn the large, flat, English- and French-style crêpes in favor of the smaller and sweeter American version.

My children have grown up thinking the latter *are* English pancakes, and it's only on Shrove Tuesdays that they realize they are not. We serve them with maple syrup and seasonal fruit, and in the past I used to make what we call "Barbie" pancakes—tiny dots that can be served to dolls and suchlike. But I had never thought of making pancake men until I reread *Little House in the Big Woods*.

> *For breakfast there were pancakes, and Ma made a pancake man for each one of the children. Ma called each one in turn to bring her plate, and each could stand by the stove and watch, while with the spoonful of batter Ma put on the arms and the legs and the head. It was exciting to watch her turn the whole little man over, quickly and carefully on a hot griddle. When it was done, she put it smoking hot on the plate.*

What chance do ordinary pancakes stand after you've tasted one of Ma's pancake men?

You can use the recipe below to make Ma's pancake men or simple, round pancakes. Either way, I can guarantee they will be enormously popular with both adults and children. I often serve these pancakes on the weekend; the batter is quick and easy to make and it doesn't need to stand before cooking.

**MAKES 8–10 PANCAKE MEN OR 20–24 ROUND PANCAKES**

*5 tablespoons butter, plus extra for greasing*
*1¼ cups milk*
*2 eggs*
*1¾ cups all-purpose flour*
*1 tablespoon superfine sugar*
*4 teaspoons baking powder*
*½ teaspoon salt*
*Maple syrup and fresh fruit, to serve*
*Flat frying pan, pancake pan, or griddle*

1. Put the butter and milk in a small pan and warm over a low heat just long enough to melt the butter. Set aside to cool a little.

2. Lightly beat the eggs in a small bowl, then add the butter and milk mixture. Stir to mix.

3. Put the flour, sugar, baking powder, and salt into a large bowl and stir with a fork to mix. Pour the egg mixture into the flour mixture and stir with a large spoon until the dry ingredients are incorporated—but don't overmix (this doesn't have to be as well mixed as a sponge cake recipe).

4. Heat the pan or griddle and butter it very lightly by running a piece of kitchen paper dipped in a tiny amount of butter over its surface.

5. To make round pancakes, ladle a spoonful of mixture onto the pan for each pancake (it's best to keep them quite small so that they cook evenly)—up to five or so at a time—and cook until the bubbles break on the surface. Flip the pancakes over and cook for another 30 seconds or until the bottoms are lightly browned. Serve immediately.

6. To make a pancake man, make a central body circle, then five smaller circles for the head, arms, and legs. You need to work quickly so that the batter runs and joins together to make a whole that can be turned over. Follow Ma and make only one man at a time, otherwise you could end up with some strange pancake creatures. Unless, of course, that is your objective.

7. Serve with maple syrup and fresh fruit such as raspberries, strawberries, or blueberries.

# *Make Snow Pictures*

**T**HERE are so many children in books doing enjoyable things in the snow that, as it becomes increasingly rare, it must be difficult for modern children not to feel very wistful and just a little sad to be missing out on so much fun.

All the more reason, then, for them to be ready with plenty of ideas for things to do when it does finally snow and they can throw themselves into enjoying it. Maybe literally, like Laura and Mary in *Little House in the Big Woods* by Laura Ingalls Wilder, who, even though they know the snow is going to stick around for the whole winter, still run outside enthusiastically with their cousins on Christmas Eve to make "snow pictures."

*The way they did it was this:*

*Each one by herself climbed up on a stump, and then all at once, holding their arms out wide, they fell off the stumps into the soft, deep snow. They fell flat on their faces. Then they tried to get up without spoiling the marks they made when they fell. If they did it well, there in the snow were five holes, shaped almost exactly like four little girls and a boy, arms and legs and all. They called these their pictures.*

I wonder how many children make a fervent wish for snow at Christmastime after reading this?

NOTE: There's another, sweet variation on this theme: If a child falls backward on the snow, then moves his arms and legs up and down before getting up, he'll make a snow angel.

# Ma's Hand-Sweetened Cornbread

*She made the cornmeal and water in two thin loaves, each shaped in a half circle. She laid the loaves with their straight sides together in the bake-oven, and she pressed her hand flat on top of each loaf. Pa always said he did not ask any other sweetening, when Ma put the prints of her hands on the loaves.*

What is the cook's equivalent of the gardener's green fingers, I wonder? How is it possible to suggest the magic touch some cooks and bakers have that makes everything they create successful and delicious? Because this is exactly what Laura's mother is blessed with and it's why I love reading how, in *Little House on the Prairie*, her hands leave both a literal and a metaphorical imprint on cornbread.

Cornbread is the staple food of the Little House family. They eat cornmeal cakes cooked on a campfire under the vast expanse of sky on their journey to the little house, and they eat cold cornmeal on their journey away from it. In between, they eat it for breakfast and supper, steaming hot, cold, plain, or flavored, and Ma is instructed to bake it when "Indians" come visiting.

There is something ineffably reassuring, homey, simple, and comforting about cornbread. It might be the everyday stuff of many American kitchens, but when you have never encountered or tasted it except when reading Laura Ingalls Wilder's books, it takes on an extraordinary dimension. Especially when it is made by Ma with her magic baking hands.

There are so many ways of making cornbread that it's impossible to give a definitive recipe, but this one makes a good-size, tasty version that is quick and easy to make and, in keeping with Ma's approach, it does not contain any sweetening ingredient such as sugar or honey.

Cornbread is often flavored, so you might want to add one or more of the following: crisp pieces of cooked bacon, a chopped fresh green chili, a couple of sliced spring onions, fried onions.

**MAKES 1 LARGE CORNBREAD (SERVES 8)**
*½ cup milk*
*6 tablespoons unsalted butter*
*2½ cups cornmeal*
*2½ cups all-purpose flour*
*2 teaspoons baking powder*
*2 teaspoons baking soda*
*1 teaspoon salt*
*1 egg*
*½ cup plain yogurt or buttermilk*
*8-inch round pan, greased with butter, the base lined with baking parchment*

1. Preheat the oven to 350°F.

2. Warm the milk in a pan. Remove from the heat, add the butter, and leave while the butter melts. Sift the dry ingredients into a large mixing bowl.

3. When the milk and butter liquid is cool, beat in the eggs and yogurt or buttermilk. Pour into the bowl and mix quickly.

4. Turn the mixture into the pan. Using a wet hand (otherwise the dough will stick), gently level the surface and press to leave an imprint.

5. Bake for approximately 25 minutes or until the top is golden and the bread is firm to the touch.

6. Turn out and cut into slices or squares. Serve hot and with a sweet smile.

# Sugar on Snow

**W**HEN I was eleven, I had to memorize the poem "Silver" by Walter de la Mare for an exam. I have never forgotten its opening lines: "Slowly, silently, now the moon, walks the night in her silver shoon," with all those soft, sibilant sounds that are so magical and evocative. The appeal of "sugar on snow," the more popular and poetic name for maple syrup candy, works on the same principle, I think, because there is something similarly wondrous about the simplicity and purity of the sounds, as well as the idea of drizzling a thin stream of hot syrup onto fresh, white snow and eating it immediately after it has been transformed into a chewy treat.

Not that Laura Ingalls Wilder calls it "sugar on snow" in *Little House in the Big Woods*—but when Grandma makes maple syrup candy, we have one of the most memorable food moments in children's literature. The very special "sugar snow" creates the ideal conditions for collecting maple sap to make syrup, and family and friends are all conscripted to help, and celebrate later with a big party at which the highlight is maple syrup candy.

Grandma boils up the syrup until it "waxes" and then, with a big wooden spoon, she pours hot syrup onto each person's plate of freshly gathered snow. In an instant it cools into candy that is eaten as fast as possible by everyone, young and old, at the party. It's all wonderful, family, snowy fun and I think it could be a great way of enjoying the special times when snow falls.

And should there ever be a really deep, thick blanket of snow, I'll be tempted to take the pan outside and fling the syrup directly onto it, and make wild patterns and swirls on the huge, blank, white canvas in a grand Jackson Pollock style.

This treat can be created quite easily in the absence of snow, although pouring the hot syrup onto crushed ice may not feel quite as poetic as flinging it over a layer of glistening, crystalline snow. Nevertheless, it's enjoyable to make, especially if you use wooden lollipop sticks to roll up the strands of sticky candy.

For a traditional and authentic sugar snow party, serve the candy with coffee, beer, doughnuts, sour pickles (gherkins), and saltines.

MAKES ENOUGH FOR 4–6 PEOPLE TO PLAY
*2 cups maple syrup*
*Clean snow or crushed ice*

1. Gather the snow on large plates (one per person) and leave outside by the back door. If you are using crushed ice, have your plateful(s) at the ready in the freezer.

2. Boil the syrup to 255°F or hard crack stage on a sugar thermometer. This will take about 6–7 minutes. If you don't have a sugar thermometer, test by dropping a small amount of the syrup into a small bowl of iced water. If the syrup forms long threads that are pliable (not breakable), the correct temperature has been reached.

3. Allow the syrup to cool for a couple of minutes so that the boiling subsides.

4. Bring in the plates from outside or retrieve from the freezer. If you are going for the Jackson Pollock effect, take the pan of syrup outside.

5. With a wooden or metal spoon, quickly drizzle strips, lines, squiggles, doodles, letters, lattices, lace, messages onto the surface of the snow or ice. Don't drop large dollops of syrup because they will melt the snow and fall through.

The syrup will be transformed on contact with the snow into a waxy, chewy candy.

6. Make maple syrup lollipops by quickly running a wooden stick along a strip and twirling it; the candy will roll up into a lollipop.

## ACKNOWLEDGMENTS

I would like to thank everyone at Perigee Books who has been involved with this book, in particular John Duff, publisher, and Jennifer Eck, managing editor, who have both done so much to help it on its way. I also want to thank my wonderful editor, Meg Leder, for her attention to detail, passion for words and books, and her good humor, all of which have made working with her a great pleasure.

Deciding which books to include was no easy task, but I was helped enormously by the readers of my blog, Yarnstorm (www.yarnstorm .blogs.com), who made many useful suggestions. Irene Vandervoort of Penguin Books in New York sent me an indispensable list of American classics, and I am very grateful for her help and advice.

My reading habits were formed early and I am fortunate that my mum encouraged me to read when I was a child, gave me complete literary freedom, and made sure I had plenty of library tickets. Thanks, Mum.

I am deeply indebted to my husband, Simon, for his unwavering support for this book from the very first inklings of the idea, for his patience and enthusiasm while I was writing it, and for dealing manfully with the large quantities of baked goods that appeared in our kitchen during recipe testing.

Most of all, I would like to thank my children: Tom, Alice, and Phoebe. It was through reading to them night after night, year after year, that I had the opportunity to rediscover many marvelous books in their company, and to make a whole host of new discoveries. Phoebe, in particular, deserves a very special thank-you for trawling through shelves of children's books in search of food references and for spending hours in the kitchen with me testing recipes and making invaluable suggestions. It has been a delight and privilege to work with her.

# BIBLIOGRAPHY

Ahlberg, Janet and Allan. *It Was a Dark and Stormy Night* (Puffin, 1996).

Alcott, Louisa May. *Little Women* (Signet Classics, 2004).

Bawden, Nina. *The Peppermint Pig* (Dell Yearling, 1988).

Blyton, Enid. *Five Go Adventuring Again* (Hodder, 2001).

——. *The Mystery of the Secret Room* (Egmont Books, 2003).

——. *The Rat-a-Tat Mystery* (Award Publications, 2009).

——. *The Secret of Spiggy Holes* (Award Publications, 2009).

Bond, Michael. *A Bear Called Paddington* (Houghton Mifflin, 2008).

Brisley, Joyce Lankester. *The Milly-Molly-Mandy Storybook* (Kingfisher, 2001).

Burnett, Frances Hodgson. *A Little Princess* (Sterling, 2004).

——. *The Secret Garden* (Signet Classics, 2003).

Byars, Betsy. *The Midnight Fox* (Faber, 2002).

Carroll, Lewis. *Alice's Adventures in Wonderland* (Penguin Classics, 2003).

Coolidge, Susan. *What Katy Did* (Dover Publications, 2006).

——. *What Katy Did at School* (ValdeBooks, 2010).

Dahl, Roald. *Danny the Champion of the World* (Puffin, 2007).

——. *Matilda* (Puffin, 2007).

Edwards, Dorothy. *My Naughty Little Sister* (Egmont Books, 2008).

——. *My Naughty Little Sister's Friends* (Egmont Books, 2008).

Fleming, Ian. *Chitty Chitty Bang Bang* (Perfection Learning, 2005).

Garnett, Eve. *The Family from One End Street* (Puffin Classics, 2004).

Grahame, Kenneth. *The Wind in the Willows* (Signet Classics, 2006).

Hedderwick, Mairi. *Katie Morag and the Big Boy Cousins* (Red Fox, 1999).

Hughes, Shirley. *Alfie's Feet* (Red Fox, 2009).

Kemp, Gene. *The Turbulent Term of Tyke Tyler* (Macmillan Publishing, 1986).

L'Engle, Madeline. *A Wrinkle in Time* (Square Fish, 2007).

Lewis, C. S. *The Lion, the Witch and the Wardrobe* (HarperCollins, 2000).

Lindgren, Astrid. *Pippi Longstocking* (Puffin, 2005).

Lovelace, Maud Hart. *Betsy-Tacy* (HarperCollins, 2000).

——. *Betsy-Tacy and Tib* (HarperCollins, 1993).

Masefield, John. *The Box of Delights* (NYR Children's Collection, 2007).

Milne, A. A. *The House at Pooh Corner* (Puffin, 1992).

Montgomery, L. M. *Anne of Green Gables* (Sterling, 2004).

Nabb, Magdalen. *Josie Smith* (HarperCollins, 2000).

Nesbit, E. *The Story of the Treasure Seekers* (Chronicle Books, 2006).

Norton, Mary. *The Borrowers* (Sandpiper, 2003).

Pearce, Philippa. *Tom's Midnight Garden* (Greenwillow Books, 1992).

Porter, Eleanor H. *Pollyanna* (Tark Classic Fiction, 2008).

Ransome, Arthur. *Winter Holiday* (David R. Godine, 1989).

Spyri, Johanna. *Heidi* (Puffin, 2009).

Stevenson, Robert Louis. *Treasure Island* (Puffin, 2008).

Streatfeild, Noel. *Ballet Shoes* (Puffin, 1973).

Travers, P. L. *Mary Poppins* (Harcourt, 2006).

——. *Mary Poppins Comes Back* (Harcourt, 2006).

Webster, Jean. *Daddy-Long-Legs* (Puffin, 1995).

White, E. B. *Charlotte's Web* (HarperCollins, 2001).

Wilder, Laura Ingalls. *Little House in the Big Woods* (HarperCollins, 2003).

——. *Little House on the Prairie* (HarperCollins, 2003).

## ILLUSTRATION CREDITS

xi, 7, 177—Enid Blyton, *The Secret of Spiggy Holes* (Basil Blackwell, 1940), illustrations by E. H. Davie. Reproduced by permission of Basil Blackwell.

xii, 183—Joyce Lankester Brisley, *The Adventures of Milly-Molly-Mandy* (Macmillan). Reproduced by permission of Macmillan Children's Books UK.

xv—Enid Blyton, *Five on a Hike Together* (Hodder & Stoughton, 1997), illustration by Eileen Soper.

10, 13—Michael Bond, *A Bear Called Paddington* (HarperCollins, 2003), illustration by Peggy Fortnum. Reprinted by permission of Harper-Collins Publishers Ltd.

19—Frances Hodgson Burnett: *The Secret Garden* (Puffin), illustration by Robin Lawrie. Used by kind permission of Puffin Books.

33—Frances Coolidge, *What Katy Did* (Puffin), illustration by Neil Reed. Used by kind permission of Puffin Books.

49—Roald Dahl, *Danny the Champion of the World* (Puffin, 2001), illustration by Quentin Blake.

55—Dorothy Edwards, *My Naughty Little Sister* (Egmont, 2002), illustration by Shirley Hughes. Used by kind permission of Egmont.

58, 62—Dorothy Edwards, *My Naughty Little Sister's Friends* (Egmont, 2007), illustration by Shirley Hughes. Used by kind permission of Egmont.

69—Kenneth Grahame, *The Wind in the Willows* (Curtis Brown), illustrations by E. H. Shepard. Reproduced with permission of Curtis Brown Group Ltd.

74—Shirley Hughes, *Alfie's Feet* (Red Fox, 2004), illustration by Shirley Hughes. Reproduced by permission of the Random House Group Ltd.

79, 82—C. S. Lewis, *The Lion, the Witch and the Wardrobe* (copyright © by C. S. Lewis Pte. Ltd., 1950), illustrations by Pauline Baynes. Reprinted by permission.

111—A. A. Milne, *The House at Pooh Corner* (Egmont, 2004), illustrations by E. H. Shepard.

145, 151—P. L. Travers, *Mary Poppins* (HarperCollins), illustration by Mary Shepard. Reprinted by permission of HarperCollins Publishers Ltd.

162—E. B. White, *Charlotte's Web* (Puffin), illustration by Garth Williams.

169—Laura Ingalls Wilder, *Little House in the Big Woods* (Egmont, 2000), illustration by Garth Williams.

179—Eve Garnett, *The Family from One End Street* (Puffin Modern Classics, 1942), illustration by Eve Garnett. Reproduced by permission of Penguin Books Ltd.

# INDEX